TABLE OF CONTE.

Preface	3
Art Williams: Part 1 - Your #1 Responsibility (1977-1979)	5
Art Williams: Part 2 - Top 200 Earners Meeting (1982-1985, 1995)	13
Art Williams: Part 3 - Hawaii Hyatt Regency (1983-1984)	43
Art Williams: Part 4 - Leadership Meetings (1984-1985, 1988)	62
Art Williams: Part 5 - Positive Winning Attitude (1984-1985)	93
Art Williams: Part 6 - Kansas City & New Orleans (1990)	108
Art Williams: Part 7 - Winning and Commitment (1985-1990)	117
Art Williams: Part 8 - "Crush You" (2007)	170
Art Williams: Part 9 - The Greatness of A.L. Williams (1996)	180
Art Williams: Part 10 - Winning Financially by Recruiting (1996)	185
History of A.L. Williams	189
Art's Memorable Quotes	192
Art's Present Day Fax Messages	200
Art Said: Wisdom From the Coach	206
Art Quotes That Got You Recruiting	214
Art's Way: The A.L. Williams System	220
Bob Miller: Characteristics of Art's Management Techniques	228
Art Williams: Having A Great Partnership in Marriage	232

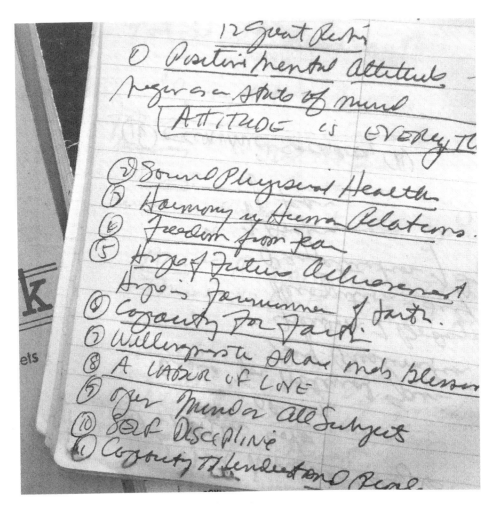

This book is sold with the understanding that the publisher and author are not engaged in rendering professional services. If assistance is required, the services of a licensed and competent professional should be sought.

References to A.L. Williams (now Primerica) are historical in nature. Primerica offers a tremendous opportunity of individuals who work hard and who desire to build a business with strong income potential.

Copyright © 2017 by Bill Orender and Orender's Champions, LLC
All rights reserved.

No part of this book may be reproduced, stored in a retrieval system, or transmitted by any means, electronic, mechanical, photocopying, recording or otherwise, without written permission from the copyright holder.

ISBN 10: 0-692-85859-8
ISBN 13: 978-0-692-85859-2
Orender's Champions Publishing: Frisco, Texas

PREFACE

ALL WE HAD WERE WORDS....

We all take notes when we think something important is being said.
I had gone to countless meetings where Art was the speaker. Then it dawned on me that his words were actually history being made. It was then that I set aside special notebooks where each time Art spoke I wrote down as much as I could.

Over 8 years I amassed 6 different notebooks. They were Steno notebooks, the kind secretaries used to take dictation from their bosses.

As Art was speaking I wrote a lot of one-liners because they were snippets of thoughts.

There are a lot of repetitive notes as Art would repeat the cornerstone and fundamental thoughts that built ALW. As Angela would say "Art has only one speech and he gives it over and over".

Understand that until 1986 when American Can Company bought out PennCorp Financial, who owned our insurance carrier, Mass Indemnity and Life Insurance Company (MILICO), our success was in doubt. We needed a company that could afford our massive growth.

At many of Art's meetings, starting in 1977, he would begin each of his talks with "We are probably not going to make it, but if we do... it will be big".

As Art's right hand man and mathematical genius, Boe Adams' job was to keep us in business. Financial Assurance was the first company we were with but they told us to leave because we were growing so quickly. We were running them out of money.

Our next company, National Home Life, told us to leave too. We had just picked a fight with the giants of the life insurance industry and no respected insurance carrier in America would touch us.

Finally, PennCorp Financial, who owned the 600th largest insurance company in America, MILICO, bet on us. American Can Company, which later became a part of Citigroup, bought PennCorp and the rest was history.

I recently saw Art and he gave an example of ALW's growth from 1977 to 1990. We started with 85 people and grew to 250,000 licensed agents. That's like the current Primerica field force of 100,000 people growing to 254,000,000 licensed in 13 years.

Most of the words you read were said while our company was in doubt as to whether we would make it. Art's words gave hope, assurance and inspiration to keep our dreams alive.

We didn't have the luxury of a "Big Sugar Daddy" company behind us. All we had was a leader who had singular vision and a fighting spirit.

When asked why we met so often, Art would say, "If we didn't meet, y'all would be committing suicide out there". "A bugler's sound must be clear so the troops don't retreat". His sound of "Charge" gave us clarity, boldness and courage. These words inflamed the cause that changed an industry and brought financial independence to millions.

Monumental is too small to describe what Art and his 85 accomplished. It was an astonishing achievement to change an industry. Against all odds, they managed to give an industry a makeover and not turn it "upside down" but "right side up".

Art is an American free enterprise icon. He is the gold standard for millions of hopefuls wanting to do something special with their lives.

Where did the 85 get the DESIRE that transcended average and ordinary? What fueled their tenacity and TOUGHNESS? There is something to be said that by working through the darkest times, something lasting is created.

The soul of the movement came from the ORIGINAL CRUSADER, ART WILLIAMS. As Norman Dacey, author of *What's Wrong With Your Life Insurance*, said in the epilogue of his groundbreaking masterpiece: "Where will the American people find a CRUSADER to stand in front of this modern day juggernaut and cry halt? Who will take the cause and do it? Will he be found in the halls of Congress or in some obscure Attorney General's office? When he takes the job and does it, he will bring more financial security to the American people than 100 years of social security".

The insurance industry was the only "Goliath" big enough for Art and his 85.

The words that are written in this book were all Art had and needed to put a fire in our bellies. His words made us feel like GIANTS!

To me, this quote explains Art best: "Most fame is fleeting. Only a few men grow larger with the passage of time but HEROES are always the exceptions." His words were all we had and his words were enough to build an empire. They bound us together at the beginning and still do today.

There is only one Art Williams.

Bill Orender

A special Thank You to Caroline Myers, Janay Brumfield, Patrick Orender and Carol Orender who helped me organize and edit my notes into this book.

Art Williams: Part 1

YOUR #1 RESPONSIBILITY

1977-1979

ART WILLIAMS: PART 1

FIRST A.L.WILLIAMS LEADERSHIP RETREAT
UNICOI STATE PARK & LODGE
MIDDLE OF 1977

This is where I asked Art why he wanted to leave ITT for Waddell & Reed. He answered, "Because they had one more level on the computer." Art understood that by having another level on the computer massive numbers of people would have the ability to override a team.   Bill Orender

ART WILLIAMS

YOUR #1 RESPONSIBILITY IS TO BUILD A TEAM.

HOW TO BUILD A TEAM
- Every player playing with one heartbeat
- Needs to have a common enemy that pulls people together - ours is trash value insurance

STEP 1 - YOU MUST HAVE A BIG GOAL AND A BIG VISION
- Destroy Trash Value
- Kick Prudential's butt - BE NUMBER 1
- Financial Independence - change your family for generations

STEP 2 - YOU MUST HAVE A PLAN
- Build an Army of Part-Timers - 90% need to be 4 to 5 Pointers
- Build a few Generals - 7 to 10 1st Generation RVPs

STEP 3 - YOU MUST DO IT FIRST
- Show it - Don't talk it
- Practice until perfect
- Field Train until the recruit is a District Leader

STEP 4 - YOU MUST DELIVER
- 1 Part-Timer that is making money & building a team
- 1 RVP making money & building a team

NOW - ACCEPT NO EXCUSES!!!

STEP 5 - COACH YOUR TEAM
- You get "The Best" out of people by:
  - Encouraging them, always be positive
  - Building Relationships

STEP 6 - MY WAY OR THE HIGHWAY
- There's "ONLY 1" Head Coach. That's ME. GOT IT?

People learn best by watching STUDS. Someone who has done it.

GET MOMENTUM
- Do things in bunches - get your team recruiting tons for 30 days
- Have emergency meetings - get team focused on breaking a record
- 30 day or 90 day blitz - "kill it" for short bursts of time
- Awards and recognition - do something special

HOW TO KEEP MOMENTUM
- Grow buy multiplication. Everybody:
- Recruit 3 directs
- Field train directs and get 3 directs for each recruit
- Drive each recruit 4 deep
- Explode your team to 81 recruits by 3x3x3x3

I HAD BEEN RUNNING......
- I coached for 3 different schools in 7 years
- I was with 2 companies in financial services - I hated corporate America. They looked down their nose at salespeople. The most important people in a company.

I HAVE STOPPED RUNNING......
- I will do it or not do it with A.L.Williams
- This is it for me. I will be a dud or a STUD.
- I ain't going nowhere. I am burning all my bridges.
- I want to Be Somebody so bad it hurt inside
- This is my chance. If I lose I am going down fighting at A.L.Williams.

I AIN'T RUNNING NO MORE!

BUILDING A TEAM IS ALL ABOUT BUILDING RELATIONSHIPS.

YOU KNOW WHAT?
- Nobody ever accomplished anything "on their own"

YOU KNOW WHAT?
- If you have ever been successful at anything, somewhere in your life somebody TRUSTED you - somebody BELIEVED in you and YOU believed in and trusted them.
    - I had many in my life - most important was Coach Taylor. He was a GIANT in my life.
    - Started working in the 5th Grade & playing for him through High School
    - Started Coaching - Sophomore at age 15

HOW DO YOU BUILD THIS KIND OF TRUST??
- You can't DEMAND **Trust**
- You can't DEMAND **Respect**
- You can't DEMAND **Loyalty**
- You can't DEMAND **Love**
- You can't FAKE **Honesty**
- You can't FAKE **Integrity**
- You can't FAKE **Belief**

HOW DO YOU GET PEOPLE TO TRUST YOU?
- You must always look for good things in people
- You must become an expert in praise and recognition

    <u>Rules for Recognition</u>:
    1. Recognize your people in front of others
    2. Be creative - t-shirts "I am Somebody", "I am a Stud." Have fun - "Cream of the Crap" recognition for mentally tough leaders who aren't delivering like they know they can.

- You can't let the LOSERS, the NEGATIVE people, the DISHONEST people, the UNETHICAL people make you LOSE FAITH in PEOPLE.
- You MUST show your people you REALLY CARE about THEM, THEIR FAMILY and THEIR DREAMS…
- You must "Love" them and "Believe" in them through GOOD TIMES and BAD TIMES
- My kids - Little Art & April Williams
    - When they make mistakes? I cry and I hurt.
    - *But I never stopped* loving and stop trusting them

COACH TAYLOR & COACH BEAR BRYANT
Taught me how to:
- Get people excited again
- Get people to believe in themselves again
- Get people to hope again
- Get people to dream again

SECOND, THIRD A.L.WILLIAMS LEADERSHIP RETREATS
UNICOI STATE PARK & LODGE
1978 - 1979

KNOW YOUR PRIORITIES

- Eliminate Meetings *(Get in the dadgum field and train)*
- Field Train New Recruits to District Leader
- Never send a New Recruit to dadgum outside sales trainers
- 90% of your New Recruits are 4-5 pointers
- 50% of your New Recruits get licensed
- Never make a sale on the first interview (no pressure)
- No cold calling - build in a best friends warm market
- Identify studs while Field Training - they become Field Trainers
- Each RVP should have 5-10 District Teams
  A District Team is:
    - A Field Trainer
    - has 5 to 10 sales each month
    - has 5 to 10 recruits each month
- Relationships - "Love on" your people (recognition, notes)

KEEP IT SIMPLE - THE A.L.WILLIAMS SYSTEM
- NEVER take a prospect to an opportunity meeting first. Always do an interview across the kitchen table first
- Always stay in a "warm market" for recruiting and sales
- New Recruit sets up the appointment with their BEST FRIEND
- New Recruit takes you to his BEST FRIENDS house so you don't get lost
- New Recruit takes you in the back door because that is where BEST FRIENDS enter a home
- Recruit the New Recruit's BEST FRIEND
- The New Recruit's BEST FRIENDS sets up appointment with his BEST FRIEND
- Recruit's BEST FRIEND recruits his BEST FRIEND and sets up appointment with his BEST FRIEND
- Do it again, again and again

YOUR KEY TO WINNING IS DESIRE AND DETERMINATION.

You must be SO FOCUSED on your <u>goal</u> and your <u>dream</u> that NOTHING/NOBODY can DISTRACT you.

UNWRITTEN LAW
- If you WANT IT bad enough
- If you're PASSIONATE enough
- If you're TOUGH enough

If you're EATEN UP with BEING SOMEBODY…YOU "CAN DO" IMPOSSIBLE THINGS.

The Life Insurance Companies, the Regulators, the Politicians… They FINALLY have met someone READY TO FIGHT! We will look them in the eye and say… "GO SCREW YOURSELF."

I WANT TO DO SOMETHING SPECIAL
- I don't want to build a company for those jokers (corporate America)
- I want THREE THINGS…
    1. To build my own company and give teammates a chance to build one too
    2. Achieve financial independence - nobody's thumb on me
    3. Build a legacy business that I can leave to my family

THIS COMPANY WAS BORN
- To destroy trash value insurance
- To recruit a different kind of person - good people, respected, families (4-5 pointers)

ALW IS NOT IMPRESSED BY
- Fancy dressers
- Pretty people
- Fancy university degrees
- Somebody born with a lot of money

ALW is BIGGER than sales. We are about HOPE, DREAMS and OPPORTUNITY. We are giving you a chance to be EXCITED AGAIN and FEEL GOOD ABOUT YOURSELF AGAIN.

THIS COMPANY IS A...
- Relationship company - clients, team, spouses
- Warm Market company - no cold calling
- Never hold people back company - NEVER
- Loves competition company - kicking the competition's butt
- DO IT FIRST company - You ALWAYS DO IT FIRST
- Training across the kitchen table company - Not at meetings
- Build RVPs company - You - 7 to 10, Help them get 7 to 10 each
- Never forget number 1 on this list

GOAL - BUILD TRUSTING RELATIONSHIPS
- THE KEY - <u>SPENDING TIME</u>
  - To get to know them
  - To get to know their family
  - To get to know the quality of their friends
- THE KEY - <u>FIELD TRAINING</u> - This is the best way to BEGIN to build great TRUSTING relationships
  - Time you spend driving together to appointment
  - Time you spend making presentations
  - Time you spend watching the recruit and their friend REACT to each other (respect etc.)
  - Look for a STUD and you really spend a lot of quality time building a friendship with them

THE BEST TRAINING IS ALWAYS FIELD TRAINING
- Coaches believe practice makes perfect. Bosses believe you learn at meetings.
- You learn best by doing
- Learn to sell
- Learn to recruit
- Learn to be a Field Trainer
- Practice your presentation until you can't fail

The right kind of recruit doesn't want to be a professional salesman.

You screw your team by bringing in professional trainers.

A COACH BELIEVES
For every one our of success on the field there is 100 hours of practicing on the field, in the weight room, and on the track getting better and getting tougher.

ALWAYS, ALWAYS, ALWAYS TALK TO YOUR PEOPLE ABOUT
- How Great this Company Is
- Selling the Dream - Our Opportunity
- How to Build a Team
- Field Train Everyone to a Team that is 4 Deep
- Going RVP and Building 7-10 RVPs
- Building Personal Relationships
- You Must Become a Leader
- How to Become a Leader and Build Leaders
- Everybody Wants to BE SOMEBODY
- This is a Best Friends, Warm Market Company
- You Win with Your Heart, Not Your Head
- Momentum
- The Crusade - Kill Trash Value Insurance
- Being a Competitor
- Toughness
- Praise and Recognition
- Get Your People Licensed
- This is an RVP Company
- Winning and a Winning Attitude

Art Williams: Part 2

TOP 200 EARNERS MEETING

(1982-1985, 1995)

ART WILLIAMS: PART 2

5/6/1982
SAN FRANCISCO SUPER SEMINAR

A.L. WILLIAMS (ALW) WAS BUILT FOR A DIFFERENT KIND OF PERSON
- They look average and ordinary on the outside but want to Be Somebody on the inside
- Victory came tough for me
- Sales came difficult for me
- When people said no it tore my heart out
- When people don't join you or quit, it tore my heart out

If you just want to make a living why should you want to go into business for yourself?
- You get into business for yourself to go forward
- Half-butts can't make it here

The key to winning is you; not the system, not the concept.

IF YOU WANT TO WIN
- Make this business personal
- Get intense
- People buy you
- You are ALW to your people

BELIEVE
- That this is the greatest opportunity in America today
- Leadership? It means just everything
- This thing has got to mean more to you than just a business
- People will not follow a dull, disillusioned, dadgum crybaby
- People want to follow excited and enthusiastic and believing people

- We took a stance on term insurance and it wasn't popular
- This is a company of destiny!
- A will to win: this is an endurance contest
- Talent is overvalued
- It's hard for smart people to be a success. They try to figure everything out.

PRETTY PEOPLE: Sophisticated types - Harvard, Princeton, Yale etc.
- They believe they are superior
- They are not willing to start at the bottom like us

- Victory goes to those who want it, not where you come from

TO BE A WINNER
- Be a Dreamer again – we've been disillusioned for so long it's hard to dream again

RONNIE BARNES – MILLION DOLLAR EARNER
- 10,000 people in his organization
- His payroll is $500,000 a month
- Has no executive training
- Are you 50%, 75%, 25% that good?

WHERE ELSE CAN SOMEONE THAT LOOKS LIKE ME AND YOU HAVE A CHANCE TODAY?
- ALW built for people like you and me. We're not impressed by your credentials.
- We will give them a chance

A SIN? A SIN IS GETTING BEAT AND GIVING UP
- 90% of people who go into business for themselves fail
- Get off the mat one more time and I'll show you a winner. The toughest kind of people.
- There is never a test to see if a person's got the goodies or not
- We don't care about what your background is or your education

THE DREAM
A guy like me who wants to Be Somebody is giving me the chance to go into business for myself. No education is required. You can build financial independence for your family.
- A chance to travel and see the world
- We sell a pot of gold at the end of the rainbow

TO WIN
- Develop a positive attitude: every day someone is always trying to tear you down; they say you can't do it.
- Find something you can commit to. First step to greatness? A total commitment.
- Got to pay the price or can you live with losing?
- Goal: reward and punish yourself
- Grow to be a whole person

PURPOSE OF ALW
- Built for a different kind of person. Give them a chance to go into business for themselves. To make and save money.

- You can quit running here
- You can Be Somebody that you're proud of here
- How do you think it would feel to be totally financially independent?
- ALW gives families a chance to be financially independent

WHAT IS THE KEY TO VICTORY? YOU!
- If you can improve you, all the rest will fall into place
- For things to get better, you've got to get better
- For things to improve, you've got to improve
- A leader wants to win
- Somehow he's going to find a way to win
- Excuses don't count in the big leagues. For big money, big success, big winning, there are no excuses
- The key is YOU. You become the kind of person people rally around.
- You be positive, excited, enthusiastic and your people will also
- A positive attitude comes with pain and agony

90 DAY PLAN
- Work on you: assets – liabilities
- Find a hero in this company and pattern your life after them, and be more like them.
- Make an effort. Work to get better.
- You ought to be a pacesetter
- No one is going to tap you on the shoulder and give you a fortune
- No one is going to drill an oil well in your backyard
- There's nothing I won't do: I want to Be Somebody so bad

- Freedom destroys most people in this business
- Expect miracles to happen
- Become a motivator

TO KEEP A POSITIVE ATTITUDE
- Keep them coming and going
- Run an RVP factory

THIS IS A BUSINESS OF EXPECTATION
- Expect to win
- Expect to recruit winners

You are only as good as your weakest link; work to be good at everything.

WINNING ATTITUDE
- Attitude is the difference between victory and defeat
- Have a good feeling about yourself: see yourself WINNING!
- See yourself as somebody you are proud of

GOALS
- Have a specific dream; have specific goals in your mind
- Write it down
- Spend time and look at it daily
- Decide the price you're willing to pay
- Make it an obsession

TO WIN AND SUCCEED
- Be a good person: sincerely love your people
- Feel yourself a part of a major event – get caught up in something greater than you
- Become an active participant
- Make this something you can get emotional about
- Be enthusiastic, confident, positive
- Be totally committed
- Sacrifice to win
- Pay the price to win
- No medicine is good unless it hurts

STAGES BEFORE TOTAL COMMITMENT
- Lying stage – everything is great
- Quitting stage – bad attitude
- Total commitment stage – I was put here to be a winner
- You won't know if it's a final commitment for 60–90 days

HAVE A WINNING ATTITUDE
- You must be with a company that you can believe in and delivers for you
- Understand the numbers aspect of this business
- Fact – most people are not going to buy or join you in business
- Everyone is not going to make it. Most people won't make it.
- You can't force people to buy or join – you just show them the program or opportunity we have
- Can't force people to make it. They've got to do it themselves.
- You are paid to prospect not to sell
- Winners win and losers lose

MY FIRST YEAR I WAS SICK, FRUSTRATED, EATEN UP WITH IT
- I took the business seriously
- All I heard was no, no, no, NO. Whatever I tried I got a NO.

- "Art, you are such a dog – you aren't any good."
- Then I paid a death claim and it all came to me. This stuff works.
- I hired somebody and he quit me. He was sharp looking, he was life licensed, and he still quit me.
- "Art, you're such a dud to recruit those kinds of people and they don't make it."
- He's the loser not you. Don't concentrate on the losers
- Live for those who stay and fight
- Mindset: Don't let the door hit you on the butt on the way out
- General Patton was average in every way. He was a leader and everyone wants to follow a leader.

STORY OF TWO RVP'S
- In the same city, same contract, same everything
- Both work hard, sacrifice, are good people, are loyal, and have product knowledge
- One goes beyond good to be great – he does everything, plus a little bit more
- He sacrifices and a little bit more
- $50,000 RVP – almost gets there, almost is a way of life for most people
- Do It – whatever it takes to get the job done
- Then they talk about how great it is to Be Somebody they are proud of and how they are not like everybody else
- There is too much talk
- Do it, do it, do it, do it, do it, do it
- I'll pay any kind of price for greatness
- Winners do it, and do it, until the job gets done!

SOMEBODY: I was put here to BE SOMEBODY SPECIAL!

ALW was built for a different kind of family, for a different kind of opportunity, for people to get into business for themselves and have a chance to make some real money, get real security, and have a real chance for success.

- Expect to succeed
- Be totally positive and totally committed

THE "DREAM OF ALW"
For less than $100 have a chance for the average family to go into business for themselves, a chance to Be Somebody, start part time, not go for broke, have a chance to build security, have a significant income and a chance to become financially independent.
ALW was built for people who are tired of being average and ordinary, tired of just getting by, just making ends meet and having more month than the money.

12/17/1982
ATLANTA, GA

HAVE A GOAL OF GREATNESS
- A life's goal should be to succeed to such a high level where others, who are successful, are compared to you.

3/14/1983

- All the real money hasn't been made yet

YOU GROW TO BE A LEADER
- That you respect
- That your company needs
- That your company deserves

- I've never given up on anyone
- No one was a better people person than Art Williams. No one has more patience with you than Art Williams.

Ingredients for a great Leader: Effort, Loyalty, Commitment, Leadership.

HOW DO YOU JUDGE A GREAT LEADER?
- By the number of great people they produce
- People like me want to Be Somebody

I'm proud to be part of a company that did great things.

TWO REASONS WE FORMED ALW
1. We built ALW to give families like mine a chance
2. A good business opportunity to accumulate and build security
   - These are the reasons we will hire anyone

- Do something great – Provide great leadership
- I feel a moral obligation to deliver for those people out there who are putting their lives on the line for us

- No one can bestow leadership. It is earned
- Losers always look outside their own hierarchy for answers
- People are going to do what they have to do to get by

Your people get on fire when you get on fire. Your people start recruiting when you start recruiting. Your people start making money when you start making money.

- Show me a winner and you will go on being a winner
- Keep calling the plays and stay after it until you win

- Some people can stay motivated for 3 to 4 months, good people 6 to 12 months, but a stud can remain motivated forever

- I want to be recognized as a stud. I want to make a contribution to ALW. To be recognized by my peers as a stud.

- You've got to be willing to do the right things to win
- It takes 3 to 4 years in management to learn to do the right things to get consistent growth

RVP PROMOTION
- If you don't hurt you won't go RVP
- If it didn't hurt giving up a replacement your up-line RVP didn't get a good replacement

- Think different: I think bigger, making lots of money, helping others make money, instead of minoring in problems.
- We need to think BIGGER. We need to think our people can do more, and expect more from them.

90% of our production comes from 10% of our RVPs.

- I want to make a difference in peoples lives
- I wasn't supposed to just exist

- I wasn't put on this earth to be a half butt
- I want to be part of something great

- I have a sincere love for the company. This is what I want to do with my life.
- I Love ALW with a devotion
- Be proud of your position
- Build a little pride in your organization. Have love, devotion, teamwork, to this company.
- Feel free to stir it up

- Manage activity in a tough minded way
- 99.9% of the time I think positive
- For things to get better you've got to get better
- Be bound and determined you are going to do it
- Build an empire to be wealthy. Be good at everything.
- Do it by doing it

Winning is learned. Being a winner is learned.

- Leadership qualities work like a magnet
- Lead by example
- Be proud of what you are and what you represent

- Be a person you want to be around.
- We have a responsibility to make people feel good
- Build on people strengths. Look at their good points.

MAKE EVERYBODY FEEL SPECIAL
- Everyone should be treated as a person you respect and want to be like
- Be a person they want to grow up to be. Be positive with your people.
- Everyone is looking for a hero
- Master the art of making people feel good with recognition
- People will live up to your expectation of them
- I wouldn't want anyone else on my team but you

ALW WAS BUILT FOR PEOPLE LIKE ME
- I don't want to live a humdrum average life. I've chosen to be controversial.
- I am not happy just getting by unless I've got a cause
- Everything in my life has led me to this moment
- We are different kind of people. We are always hungry.

- Some people are put on this earth to do something special and contribute
- Because of our people we can never throw in the towel
- Our people motivate us

TALENT IS A LIABILITY
- Talent is not the key. This company will never stop believing in you.
- We built this company for somebody who wants to Be Somebody
- Leadership is earned
- Life will give you whatever you'll fight for and take
- You can't just show up to work. You've got to suck it up.

- No one outside of ALW will ever have a say about this company but us and our kind of people
- I want to do something great, record breaking, the worst that can happen is there will be people who produce and will make a lot of money
- I just don't want to be a half butted organization, mediocre, average and ordinary. I want to do something great.
- I want this organization to Be Somebody. I want you to Be Somebody.

The day you decide that you and your family deserve better, deserve Hawaii, deserve Europe, deserve the home of your dreams... that day you become a winner.

5/28/1983

ARE YOU TOUGH ENOUGH?
- If you are tough enough and believe enough you can make it in ALW
- I love you and I love your excitement about our company
- A Championship season: A few teams have a chance to stand apart
- Common ingredient is a killer instinct, a knockout punch. To be number one forever.

ALW IS KNOCKING OUT THE COMPETITION
- We took the complexities out of life insurance
- We do what is right 100% of the time
- ALW doesn't want anything but an opportunity to compete. We're busting records in the hardest industry in the last 50 years.

- We don't need better products, prospects, commissions, support: we need a kick in the butt. No excuses. If you do have excuses then you don't deserve to win.
- Toughness: America has lost its toughness

THREE THINGS WILL BE REALITY IF WE LIVE LONG ENOUGH
1. Look people in the eye and tell people ALW is for real.
   - We are here forever – to deliver for your family
   - I want to Be Somebody
   - People want us to tell it like it is, but say "Please deliver if I do."
   - If you do it we will deliver. I promise you. We Will pay off for your family.
2. Pay off for the right kind of people not prima-donnas
   - ALW built for a different kind of people. People who had it stuck to them.
3. ALW sticks it to the competition. Free enterprise and unfair competition.
   - Now is the time to join ALW – everything is right

KNOW YOUR PURPOSE FOR GOING INTO BUSINESS
Your Purpose is Independence:
- Be your own boss, Build financial independence for your family
- Make money and save money
- Build security for your family
- If all you want to do is make a living you are crazy to get into business for yourself.

Go for it – let it rip, make real money, save money, don't stop until you do.

THIS IS THE GREATEST MONEY MAKING OPPORTUNITY
Why is it so great? Because it is so tough!
- Very few people want to win – to make money, have freedom.
- 98% don't want it bad enough. They want to win only if they don't have to be on commission, if it's easy.
- 2% are eaten up with it. They know they were put on this earth to Be Somebody.
- AL Williams was built for people who want to Be Somebody

I don't know why I am like I am but my butt is always burning!

TO WIN
1. Expect to Win – expect a victory
   - Develop an attitude of great expectation
   - Tell your kids they are special
   - You live up to your expectations
   - Just know you will succeed and you will
   - See yourself winning. See yourself on top the scoreboard
2. Good feeling about what you were doing. Not the money, we are doing it for people.
3. This business has to become emotional to you
   - I Wish you could go carry a death claim
   - You just can't hope you are right
   - Deliver to a Widow a $100,000 check and you'll get tough and bounce back from defeat

- To make money just means everything. We have the best part-time opportunity in America.
- I am no longer worried about what other people think
- This is really a prestigious kind of business

You've got to get excited if you want to win. You need to make a commitment.

FOUR THINGS WE'VE GOT
1. Awesome financial backing of American Can
2. Products – products of the future
3. Better way to build a company:
   Part time –
   - A better quality of person comes from part-timers
   - No sales experience and no pressure sales because people don't have to be full-time
4. Awesome administrative support

VICTORY
- Victory came very difficult for me. I found out what it takes to win. Not talent.
- It takes a Will to Win – to be eaten up with it
- Winners know they were put here to Be Somebody
- Hard for smart people to make it in America. They are paid for what they know not what they do.
- Pretty people – aren't willing to do what we do. They never had it hard.

HOW TO WIN
- Become a Dreamer again
- Look in the dadgum mirror. If you don't change, nothing will change
- Get excited, turned on, and positive again, like you used to be
- Get after it one more time, dream one more time

REALIZE THE AWESOMENESS OF ALW
- We have a chance to do something great
- Where else are people like you and me going to have an opportunity like this?

UNDERSTAND
- This company built for a different kind of person
- Grunts –who look like me. We don't care who you are, where you come from.

- People fear that if you failed in business you are branded a loser all your life
- It's not a sin to get beat. It's a sin to give up.
- Winners want to "Be Somebody"
- They don't throw in the towel, they go for it one more time

- Throw up: Corporate America - if you go for an interview with a big corporation, a top a job that you want; can you qualify for it? They trash can your resume.

- You can Be Somebody in A.L.Williams
- You have a chance
- Just put on the helmet and you have a chance

COACHING
- Learn how to suck it up
- Learn how to win
- Learn how to lead people
- These are the important things in American business

WE SELL A DREAM
The dream is giving people like me and you, who want to Be Somebody, a chance to go into business for yourself, become a Regional Vice President, make real money, have real financial security and real financial independence, and travel all over the world.
We sell Hope, a dream, an opportunity, and a pot of gold at the end of the rainbow.

AMERICA IS STARVING FOR GOOD LEADERS
- Motivators – enthusiastic, turned on human beings
- Do It – too much training and too much talking; do whatever it takes
- Winner – stays motivated for as long as it takes to get the job done

Leadership is everything. Get turned on, enthusiastic, people won't follow a dull, disillusioned, dadgum crybaby.

- We are free enterprisers to the core. We give no handouts.
- Politicians have sold us out

THESE THINGS DESTROY PEOPLE IN BUSINESS
- Fear of the competition and perfectionism
- Competition. You can't worry about the competition. They are a bag of hot air.
- Being Controversial. Worrying about what other people say. Instead of being proud of you they try to pull you down.

Winners don't worry about things they can't control. 99% of things we worry about never happen.

- Go out and make yourself happy
- Our idea of success – no one in the insurance business ever had real success
- Think like a Head coach

- Positive attitude: you can totally screw up and still win. People will follow you.
- Look at life two ways: a beautiful experience or bad news
- No one or nothing is going to get me down. I'm going to be excited, happy, enthusiastic.

I AM ONLY HERE FOR A FLICKER AND I WANT TO BE SOMEBODY
- When your time comes – "no, not me."
- You'd better get after it. You need to compete.
- Find something you can commit to
- To make a total commitment
- Find a company you can fall in love with
- Make a real commitment to your dreams
- Pay the price – there is no free lunch

- Can you live with losing, not making money, not saving money, doing for your family, not being somebody? If yes, you will never win.
- You have to be eaten up with it
- Get up in the morning when you are so tired and get after it

HAVE A GOAL OF EXCELLENCE
- There is a price you have to pay for greatness
- You can't just show up to work

Life will make you average and ordinary if you'll take it…
You can't just keep taking it.

BE A WHOLE PERSON IN EVERY AREA OF YOUR LIFE
God First, Family Second, A.L.Williams Third
- All my life I've always wanted to Be Somebody
- I've always looked back with regret. I would do things differently.
- I made up my mind I was going to go for it. I quit running. I've stopped running. I'm settling right here.
- Make a lot of money
- I was put here to Be Somebody

6/9/1983
OKLAHOMA CITY, OK

If you don't quit, there is always a chance.

TWO KEYS TO VICTORY
1. Expect to Win – every time, to be successful and prosperous.
2. Always do Something – do all the dumb things to have a few great things happen to you.
    - You get killed playing defensive and not calling a play

The game is not over until the game is over: For you it may be over in the next 3 to 5 years.

- I only have one shot to do something great
- I spent my whole career before ALW saying to myself "I'm a dud." I just wasn't getting a fair shake.
- It came so tough for me. I learned some great lessons.
- Can't worry about the competition
- Somehow I'm getting better. It looks hopeless right now. But I just didn't know what to do and eventually I passed them.

- ALW built for a different kind of person. One who wants to be free. Not built to help people to just make a living.

- All who join ALW never really thought they could make it big
- Life is one frustration after another

It's how you deal with those frustrations that determine the outcome of your life.

ALMOST: Most people almost get to the point where they are almost good, almost make it, then they flounder. They never quite get over the hump.

THE PETER PRINCIPLE – Go beyond being comfortable. Go on and do something great.
- Leaders don't get down
- Leaders don't get depressed
- Professional – the ability to hide those frustrations. Hide it. Always be happy and always be tough even when you don't feel like it.
- I wanted to quit every day. I hated to prospect, but I love this business. I love competing.

YOU ARE THE KEY - For things to get better you get better. For things to change you change. For things to become more positive you become more positive. Don't feel hurt. Don't quit.

Most leaders try to get others to do it. I developed a do it first mentality. Whatever you want your people to do, you do it first.

- Want people to like you? You like them first.
- You can't instill leadership. You can't make people follow you.
- Leadership is earned – become the person people want to become like

- Nothing more important than your attitude
- Find yourself a hero. Apply these principles to your life every day
- Leadership is all learned
- Develop a real love for your people, your profession, your company
- Be very proud of what you are all about

- It is worthwhile dedicating your life to doing something special
- Takes an incredibly small number of things to go right to build an empire
- Praise your people, don't jump in their mess
- Tell them every day how special they are

Systems, gimmicks are not the key. It's you. Your leadership.

- You become somebody your people can believe in
- You're looking at somebody who really wants to win
- Winning – you and your family have real money, build real security
- ALW was born for you and your people to have real success
- Everyone has a chance to get to the top
- A Winning Attitude is getting it up one more time

You are going to live with what you do in the next 12 months for years to come. That's scary. It keeps me from getting complacent. I've got everything it takes to win. But I've got to grow up.

- Winning is tough, life is tough. Just don't give up on anybody
- Expect miracles to happen in your business

- If you are a winner you can stand the heat
- There is always an answer. Just don't give up mentally.
- There is always an answer for a winner

- Don't be content with just getting by
- I want you to have the same kind of success Angela and I have had

HOW WONDERFUL IT IS TO BE DIFFERENT
I am controversial and different and I'm proud of it. Because this kind of person makes a difference in the lives of others.

- You've got to love this company, its people, what it stands for, the opportunity and what it means to future widows, families, and the self esteem of others.
- We've got to deliver for those we have committed to
- This is a serious business. We can all be very wealthy in the next 4 to 5 years.

NUMBERS ASPECT - UNDERSTAND THESE TRUTHS
- Not everyone is going to buy
- Not everyone is going to join
- You can't force people to make it
- You get paid to prospect. Take your story to enough people.

WINNERS WIN AND LOSERS LOSE
- Losers think they are the only people who have problems.
- Winners just don't quit. They work through their problems until they make it.

- My first year I was sick every day. I tried everything to win. Nothing worked. I heard no, no, no. Learn to live for the yeses.
- Change your thinking
- Quitters are duds, not you
- You've got to live for the people who want to do it. Who want to Be Somebody.
- It takes intensity to make it
- You have to work with a positive attitude every day

I PROMISE YOU TWO THINGS
1. I'll go out with you as long as it takes for you to win
2. I'll give you my time -
   - I won't give you my money
   - I won't quit on you

I want to Be Somebody. I was put on this earth to Be Somebody. I'm doing it with ALW.

Leaders move themselves best when times are tough.

Your reps know when you're committed.

"Art, You can count on me!" Great... Just do it.

FOR ONE TIME IN YOUR LIFE YOU OWE IT TO YOURSELF TO GO FOR IT
- You don't have to be just a number
- If you're rare, if you're special, you can Be Somebody you are proud of

8/12/1983
BOCA RATON, FL

LEADERSHIP
- Be the right kind of leader to this company, to your people
- Build successful people. Make people feel special. Don't use intimidating tactics. It brings out short term results.
- The greatest joy in life is pulling them through. Hoping they become somebody they are proud of.
- Deal with people the way you want to be dealt with

- I expect you to consider the person, to be honest, be above board, have integrity with every decision that you make
- Be positive, be a dynamic influence
- Develop a do it first mentality. Don't ask your people to do things you won't do.
- Recruiting is the lifeblood of this business

BUILD A STRONG BASE
- Build 7–10 RVPs and live with them every day
- Have a heavy emphasis on fast start schools

PROMOTIONS
Never make exceptions on promotions. Keep them coming and keep them going. Recruit, recruit, recruit! This thing was built for people who want to Be Somebody.

MANAGERS MANAGE THINGS BUT LEADERS LEAD PEOPLE
- There's no possibility that ALW won't be here for you and your people
- We have everything it takes to win
- ALW was built for people who want to Be Somebody
- This is my moment of opportunity
- Have a goal of making a sale a day

Folks, don't miss this boat. I don't care how much you are hurting or doing without. Dadgummit, that's the way it's supposed to be. You are trying to get to the big leagues. You want to do something great with your life. Now is the time to do it.

ALW was built for people to do something. To make a difference. To do something great and Be Somebody that they are proud of. Let's change the world – why not us? Let's make a difference in the lives of other people.

11/2/1983

- There are people who do so much, so quick in business that it can make you feel like a loser
- I want to win in all aspects of my life
- I want to see my people win, professionally, personally, family. It's becoming a reality.

- You manage on a minute by minute basis

- We're growing, learning, stretching, making mistakes
- The worst thing that is going to happen is we are going to produce a lot of millionaires
- We built ALW to be honest with you

I want to Be Somebody so bad it borders on being an obsession. I'm paranoid about Being somebody.

- I work at being positive
- Don't call me a mealy-mouth

Selling is not where it's at. I want to be financially independent. I have to build a business to be financially independent.

- We've already produced 40 to 50 millionaires in the company. We're delivering financial independence.
- Winners have got to recognize the moment they're in and go for it
- People just think they are working hard
- There is an incredible price you've got to pay to be big
- You've got to work hard and pay a phenomenal price

I was sick and tired of being disappointed in ALW and in my life. I made up my mind it was time to quit running.

I want this to pay off for those who decide to stay and make it happen.

1983 - AVERAGE RVP EARNINGS
1st year - $74,000
2nd year - $128,000
3rd year - $218,000

Your Dream provides proper direction for you and your future.

SALES VS. RECRUITING
- I don't like selling for a living. I don't like to depend on someone saying yes or no.
- Prospecting and selling is a necessary evil
- To be a superstar from selling is pure hell. No security for your family. You've got to build an organization.

HAVE A RECRUITING MINDSET
- This is a numbers business: income long range is related directly to recruiting.
- Full-time? Recruit one person per week.
- I love it. I love building. This is why I was born.
- Two ways to make sales: get referrals – make a sale, get a recruit - make a sale.
- Recruit one recruit then they'll buy the product from you
- Recruiting must become a way of life
- Recruit every client. Recruit everyone you meet.
- If you can walk, breathe and talk I'm going to recruit you
- Greatest way to keep positive attitude is to keep them coming and going
- Not one problem can't be solved by recruiting someone

You've got to embarrass your wife several times a week because you're recruiting everybody you talk to.

Work hard: Be a diehard, be a madman, be a tornado, be a twister.

FUNDAMENTALS:
- Selling
- Recruiting
- Prospecting
- Mental preparation, mindset
- Management referral system, promotions
- Field training
- Manage activity, recruiting, appointments and presentations
- Surprise Contests
- Opportunity Meetings

YOU DO IT FIRST, PEOPLE WON'T FOLLOW A MEALY MOUTH
- Put blinders on, your people will start doing it when you start doing it
- Your life can change for the better in 90 days
- Make a 90 day commitment. A 90 day charge – no matter, good or bad, it gets you charging. You grow in plateaus.

- I want to Be Somebody
- I don't always like this business but I like the results I get
- Lots of people doing a lot of things together
- I'm sick of being average and ordinary. This is the thing that brings discipline to your life.

BURN ALL BRIDGES
This is Life or death, a "burn all your bridges" kind of commitment. Let it rip!

I live for those who believe. Who want to stay and fight. Not for those who won't work. Who won't pay the price.

I CAN TAKE ANYTHING BECAUSE I HAVE A DREAM
- Lose sales, lose reps, lose managers, sacrifice, do without, work hard, because of the dream? I don't care because I've got a dream.
- I know what I want to be and this business is all I've got to get me there
- Go look in the mirror
- Success comes to those who want to Be Somebody more than anything else in this world
- I have developed a phenomenal positive attitude

- We are positioned for great growth. ALW is for real
- Pays off for a different kind of person
- Who else would hire us as executives. Those jokers program people to think you have to be pretty, have a degree, be smart. It's impossible for smart people to make it big in the United States. Smart people spend their whole life trying to figure things out.

- Pretty people can't make it because they were born with a silver spoon in their mouth. They think they are superior to what we are.
- 99% of superstars look, talk, and act like me

- We were too naïve not to make it
- We just do it no matter what
- We give everybody an opportunity

KEY TO OUR SUCCESS?
- We understand people
- We give you a chance if you want to try because we are different just like you are
- Learn how to suck it up when the going will get tough
- Learn how to fight

ONLY HERE FOR A FLICKER
- Is how long you're here in relation to time in general
- Attitude is everything
- You criticize yourself when they tell you no. Don't do that.
- It's a will to win. Not talent, not education, not experience,

- You need to be eaten up with it. You need to be tired of being average and ordinary.
- You are supposed to Be Somebody
- I stood for something, I made a difference
- I have an unbelievable desire to Be Somebody
- You can't wait for someone to discover you. You have to create it
- In America - you, and only you, determine your own destiny
- No one is going to find an oil well in your backyard
- We lay it all on the line
- We do something that most people won't do

QUIT FEELING SORRY FOR YOURSELF
- Be a leader
- No one will believe in you until you believe in you
- No one will do it for you
- You can't go to college and learn to win

TO WIN
- Get serious
- Get Intense
- People won't follow a mealy-mouth

BE HONEST WITH YOURSELF
- Go off by yourself and look in the mirror and be honest
- Find 2 to 3 things you least like about yourself and try to improve them
- Go find yourself a hero and copy him
- Wake up each day and give yourself a pep talk in the mirror

CHARACTERISTICS OF WINNERS
1. They are self-made
2. Become a dreamer again - *Think and Grow Rich* , page 36
3. I wrote down goals
4. I got turned on about life
5. See yourself winning, making a contribution, being someone that you're proud of
6. Get excited one more time, believe in yourself one more time
7. They look in the mirror and are honest with themselves
8. Look at the last five years. It won't change.
9. Set goals and picture success
10. Develop a Positive attitude. We are not born with a winning attitude.
11. Be an incurable optimist. Attitude is everything.
12. Stay motivated for as long as it takes to win

LIFE - YOU EITHER MAKE IT A PAIN IN THE BUTT OR A WONDERFUL EXPERIENCE
- I quit running. I'd had it.
- I'm going to spend the remaining years of my life being positive, a stud, standing for something, trying all I can
- Wear out not rust out

DEVELOP AN ATTITUDE - EXPECT TO SUCCEED
- Expect to win
- Work at it for years
- Expect your people to win
- Expect miracles
- Life will wind up the way you expected it to
- Life is a self fulfilling prophecy
- I expect everyone around me to win
- They'll all be financially free

I RUN AN RVP FACTORY
- Every new recruit, I look at them and expect him to be an RVP
- If you don't want to Be Somebody get out now
- Be good or be gone
- I expect you to win big
- I expect you to Be Somebody
- If you don't want to win, I don't want to be around you
- This company was built so you can stop running

TOTAL COMMITMENT - THE FIRST STEP TO GREATNESS
- Go whole hog
- You can't live an average and ordinary existence again
- Marriage also demands total commitment
- In life you can't have anything that has no friction, problems, etc.

BETTER FIND A BUSINESS YOU CAN COMMIT TO OR PAY THE PRICE
Everybody wants to win. They all say it but...
- 98% don't want it bad enough. They don't want to sell to do it.
- 2% are eaten up with it just like me.
- Learn how to pay the price. Life doesn't roll over and play dead. It's going to try to knock your head off. Life gives you what you'll accept and are willing to fight for.
- You will be poor and unhappy if you don't accept it and be determined to win
- Winners do everything the losers do but they do a little bit more
- A winner wants to be a superstar

Gary Player: Golf Legend
"Hey Gary you can really hit a golf ball. I'd give anything if I can hit a golf ball like you."
Gary responds, "No you wouldn't. You won't hit a golf ball till your hands bleed like me. Nothing good comes easy. Without a big price there is no pay off"

- Establish the right kind of priorities: God, family, your business
- Got to grow to be a successful person in all areas of your life
- All my life I wanted to Be Somebody
- Everything I've done, I'm ashamed of it. If I could live my life over, I would work harder.
- I was tired of being disappointed in me… Art Williams

I was so sick and tired of second guessing myself, I decided to go for it.

I WISH FOR YOU
- Be a dreamer again
- Have a goal of greatness
- Be pumped up again
- Be a leader, be financially independent
- Be excited again
- To see yourself winning
- To change your life in 90 days

- All your life you'll have others tell you that you can't do it
- Try just one more time. If it turns out bad not all is done in your life, look in the mirror and say at least say you tried. Then go try again.

11/8/1983
DALLAS, TX

TOP 200 EARNERS MEETING

- I know we are going to win. You can't defeat a will to win.
- Position can't make a person. You can't make a person an RVP or NSD. Happiness comes from within. The person makes the position.
- You have an opportunity to look back and be proud of yourself
- You need to capture the moment
- "Burn out" is just loser talk

THE TIME IS NOW
- Charge – Go for it
- Recruit big numbers
- Knock out the competition. Make big money.

I don't like sales, I like RECRUITING

THERE ARE TWO THINGS, IF YOU DO THEM, I DON'T CARE ABOUT YOU ANYMORE
1. When you have a bad attitude   2. When you quit

I don't look at any RVP that I don't expect to become financially independent out of this.

CHOICES TO MAKE
Rich and powerful and a meaningful part of this company or average and ordinary

People that lose are never honest with themselves. They think someone else lied to them.

It is impossible for a STUD to be left behind.

SELL PEOPLE ON A SERIES OF 90 DAY COMMITMENTS
- I can do anything for 90 days
- Management is different from sales. Management is a series of plateaus.
- Results come after weeks and months of preparation
- Change your life in 90 days
- Build a recruiting mentality in your business
- All great leaders in my life have an attitude of doing whatever it takes to make it go, to win.
- Nothing is beneath what a leader will do
- To win a championship your chances of winning are only as good as your weakest link. What is the weakest part of your game?

WHY DON'T PEOPLE GET TO THE TOP?
- They don't really believe the opportunity is there. They don't really commit to it.
- They don't really believe they can do it
- If you want to win, sell the dream every day
- Reinforce the opportunity…one more time
- Praise and love your people and they'll die for you

- A Crusader has an enemy. A Crusader has as a cause.
- Be the hardest worker, you've got a lot of people counting on you

ONLY ONE WAY TO MEASURE SUCCESS: THE SCOREBOARD, IT'S MONEY MADE
- 90% of being beaten on the scoreboard are problems with the fundamentals:
    - Selling and recruiting
    - Recruiting and selling
    - Prospecting and setting appointments

Turn your sales force over every 90 days.

SELL THE DADGUM DREAM!!!

FRUSTRATED AGENTS
- They really don't believe they'll be a key person, that it will pay off for them
- Jealousy and envy are negative. These come quickly after doing without goals for so long.

If you believe you are going to win, everything else will take care of itself.

You've got to believe you're going to do something SPECIAL first.

- More than anything in my life, I want this to pay off for you and your family. I love people.
- This thing is something special to me
- Most companies talk a good game, but this company delivers
- We're playing with people's lives, their futures

1984

WINNING IS A LONELY TRIP
- Everyone's telling you not to work so hard
- Can you live with yourself if you lose?
- Head coach has to live with the scoreboard. It's a total reflection on him.
- It's his decision, commitment, vision, reason for being, it's his effort, his self-esteem
- I resent someone else trying to place their values on me
- I resent average and ordinary people ridiculing my ambitions

- I resent those whose dreams are small and change a lot, ridiculing me and putting my vision down as a workaholic or not caring about my family
- I resent those who are self righteous. Those that look their noses down at me, shrug their shoulders, shake their heads, let out a little disgusted laugh and ridicule my desire, my ambition, my goals, my destiny
- Maybe you can understand why I work like I work. Why my fanaticism? Because you don't understand my reason for being, my destiny, why I was put on this earth.
- Don't impose your beliefs on me. Don't insinuate that I don't love my family or my God or life, because I have a vision.
- I'm not sure whether I can live with myself if I don't accomplish my dreams.

WINNING IS TO ME
- Where you can dream big and dedicate your life to something. Then you have to fight life, friends, family, and those lost souls who ridicule your desires.

7/1/1984

A.L.WILLIAMS WAS BORN FOR YOU AND YOUR FAMILY
- Your future
- Your dreams
- Your children's education
- Your new homes
- Your new cars

A.L.WILLIAMS IS A WAR AGAINST THE TYRANNY OF MEDIOCRITY
- Against the shame of being broke
- Against the prison of fear
- Against the prison of anxiety caused by a lack of money
- Against the prison of anxiety caused by a corporation that dictates your life
- Corporations dictate where you live, what you drive, what your children wear, whether or not your wife works, whether or not you will retire in dignity, where you go on vacation, whether or not you'll help charitable causes, they dictate your self esteem, and your self worth.
- They do this by how much they pay you

Robert Louis Stevenson: "To be what we are, and to become what we are capable of becoming, is the only end of life."

- Would you rather be someone else? Forget it.
- You have control of your life
- You have all you need to win right now
- Take credit or blame for your performance. No one else has done anything to you.
- Take full credit or full blame for your marriage. She has nothing to do with it. She just responds to you.
- The only person you can change is yourself

A.L.Williams – We relieve people and families from financial oppression. That's why there will always be an A.L.Williams.

WINNING
- Is an Attitude
- It is a Commitment
- Is a Vision of your future
- Is a Goal set and achieved
- A Symbol of your expectations
- A way of Life
- A way of Tracking how you are doing
- A Positive Reinforcement
- A Faith in your future
- A Mental Discipline
- A Personal Affirmation
- Is Dynamic, creates ideas and will power
- Is what Life is All About
- Winning cannot be ignored
- Determined by how much you earn
- Determined by how much you produce
- Determined by the leaders you produce
- Takes patience and will be accomplished if you resolve to win and see yourself winning, your belief in self
- Means you want to Be Somebody
- Means you want to be number one in your city, organization, state
- Means you're tired of losing
- It's shown in your conviction
- Means you are no longer average and ordinary
- Means Doing It
- Means willing to do the nasty things over and over

12/17/93
ATLANTA CONVENTION

IN 1977 I CHOSE TO GIVE ALW ALL I HAD
- I made mistakes along the way
- We were good at keeping our eyes on the main thing
- We would fuss and fight, but kept our long range focus
- Victory was our goal
- Winning was the end
- Any cancer in your company comes from small thinking

Art Williams: Part 3

HAWAII HYATT REGENCY

1983-1984

ART WILLIAMS: PART 3

11/9/83

HOW TO LEAD YOUR PEOPLE
- Treat people in your organization like your children
- You can't ever do anything bad enough to have me stop loving you
- Unconditional love and belief
- Big time management? You can't panic.
- Look at their paychecks to see how they are doing
- I don't know a millionaire that isn't insecure
- Always have a positive atmosphere, always
- I get emotional thinking about our people
- We need to care about them

COMMON CHARACTERISTICS OF SUCCESSFUL PEOPLE
- They work hard
- Have an unbelievable desire to Be Somebody, somebody different, somebody special.
- All I can do is work hard
- In working hard everything falls into place
- The key to my success is me. Others will let you down, I'm the only one I can really count on.
- No matter what happens to me in my life I'm going to win and I'm going to be happy
- I'm like a madman
- A head coach lives with his record the rest of his life
- Have a "you do it first" philosophy
- Be the hardest worker and the most dedicated

WHAT PEOPLE WANT IN THEIR LEADER
- People want to follow a leader
- People want to be around happy, excited, people
- We are all on a pedestal
- You have an image to your people. People look at you differently.
- When you slip up, it hurts your people
- You are their hero - you help them recruit

WHERE DOES A LEADER GO FOR MOTIVATION?
- The only thing that controls your future is you. We can be selling vacuum cleaners and be successful.
- The biggest challenge is to build leaders who are heroes to their people
- I want to be a hero
- You can't live with yourself thinking you let your people down
- You can only achieve it by being better

KEY TO BEING A HERO
- Understand your job never changes
- You are forever a District Manager
- When you stop, it stops
- Doing the same things today as you did the day you started
- The position doesn't make the man, the man makes the position
- The job never changes
- Continue to grow every day and keep rebuilding

- Find something you can dedicate your life to
- Look at your job as never changing
- Smart people go down the tubes in this life
- Keep doing the things like a district manager and you'll keep going to the top. Doing the same things over and over and over and over again.
- Grind it out

Key to the future is SELLING THE DREAM.

HOW TO DEAL WITH THE FRUSTRATIONS THAT COME WITH LEADERSHIP
- Have a great attitude
- Get into a routine every day
- Do anything to help the team win
- Heroes always do a little bit more and extra but with love and care
- There's nothing I'm too proud to do

LEADERSHIP
- It all takes care of itself if you really believe you're going to win
- If you really see yourself winning nothing bothers you so badly
- Doing within while you're doing without
- Be an example
- You do it first
- Become a dreamer
- Have a positive attitude
- Expect to succeed
- Have a total commitment
- Pay the price
- Have the right priorities
- Leaders are made not born
- You've got to be good to your people
- Be a person that loves people and make them feel special
- Art Williams realizes how insecure we all are
- I want people to say… "Art Williams made me feel special from day one. He made me feel that I was special and different. That I was not average and ordinary."

- This is my life. This is why I was born. I was born to make a difference.

OUR JOB IS TO PRODUCE SUCCESSFUL RVPS
- RVPs built ALW on loyalty
- Can't build loyalty and commitment in your people overnight
- Loyalty is not built with words but with your actions
- Do your people feel that way about you?
- Do you have unconditional love and belief in your people?
- Our job is to make people feel good
- Human nature does not allow you to blame yourself for your failures, so we blame others, especially our people
- Our job, day after day, is to keep selling this dream

The biggest problem with people? They don't believe in themselves. They can't see themselves winning, achieving, doing something special with their life.

- This is a numbers business
- We all feel, "I was put here to do something special with my life."
- We are sitting on the best business opportunity in America

ATTITUDE
- Look for ways to promote people
- Our job is to build RVPs and make people feel special and important
- Always stay a district manager
- To get to the top, build leaders and they'll push you to the top
- You be a winner, you make money, you be selling, you be the one who is always believing
- Create an attitude and atmosphere that they are part of a team
- Always be looking for good things in people

12/14/1983

TO WIN
- Believe and make a total commitment, believe without a shadow of doubt, that you're going to do it
- Have the right kind of priorities: Helping people
- It is and it isn't the money
- You judge a great man by how many people they help become successful
- Have a great attitude and bust your butt for your people

- If you base your business strictly on the personal money you make, you can't stay motivated long enough
- I believe you've got to be a crusader. You can't believe it or love it unless you're a crusader
- There are days every month when I want to quit. That's just life.
- My crusading attitude keeps me going
- You can't win unless you have a cause
- Our product and purpose is to eradicate whole life from the face of the earth

PREPARE TO WIN BIG - 3 THINGS
1. Become a Crusader
2. Have fun in the business. I love this business.
    - Fun to me is winning, making money, being somebody that you are proud of, being promoted, helping people
    - Saving money is fun
3. Just before you go to sleep think of your goals, your dreams, what you want to accomplish.
    - Have a dream to dominate the industry
    - We have a chance to make history
    - We are proud to play on a national championship team. To be among the best. To be the number one organization in the world.

- We are proud of the controversy we have generated
- I enjoy being different. People like me and you want to stand for something.
- I love being different.

- If you raise your head, they will try to knock your head off. That's why we succeed.
- Successful people never see their business changing. They never look at their job changing. They always look at it as you are a district manager.
- Winners never quit their routine
- If you ever lose your mental and physical toughness, it's hard to get it back. Continue to work hard.

I'm scared to quit recruiting, training, prospecting.

- It's so hard to get it up one more time
- ALW is key to your dream becoming a reality
- Have an attitude and do anything to help this company survive
- The group dynamics here are incredible
- The more you give the more you will receive

The number one responsibility? Building disciples and leaders forever.

NEVER SEE YOUR ROLE CHANGING
- The day you begin to change your role, you begin to die. The probability of recapturing the edge again is very rare.
- Expect miracles to happen
- Self talk is always "I can"
- Reward and punish yourself

2/21/1984

DEVELOP 6 CHARACTERISTICS TO WIN
1. Winners do everything they are supposed to do and a little bit more
2. Dream and be excited about life
3. Have a positive attitude
4. Expect to succeed
5. Make a total commitment. Pay the price: Life will give you what you will fight for.
6. Be a whole person and have the right priorities

SPEAKER - ANGELA WILLIAMS

DREAMS
- Always upgrade them
- Translate money goals into heartfelt desires
- You can be effected by the dreams of your spouse. They may be lesser or greater.
- Everyone is capable of achieving their dreams if you work hard
- Real life dreams and daydreams are not the same

Be careful of what you dream for because you'll get it.

YOUR DREAMS
- Providing for your family like you would like to
- Keeping your family together
- Dream the little things, like flying first class, having private massages, the ability to handle financial emergencies

STAGES WE GO THROUGH
- Maybe we can do it
- Dreams do come true

- You have a responsibility to give to other people, to help them fulfill their dreams
- The ultimate dream? To Be Somebody.

WHAT ARE THE REASONS ALW IS WHAT IT IS TODAY?
- God
- Our special people
- Art Williams efforts

**4/11/1984
HOUSTON, TX
RVP MEETING**

SPEAKER - ART WILLIAMS

MOST PEOPLE DO 95% OF THE RIGHT THINGS TO WIN…
THE SUPERSTARS ALSO DO THE OTHER 5%
- They show up to work every day, and work when everyone else is quitting
- This is an endurance contest, grind it out, over and over again
- Winning? There is no alternative in ALW.
- Victory will go to those who want to Be Somebody
- This company will never disappoint the right kind of person
- Give people the benefit of the doubt
- Don't be suspicious of everybody
- Look for the good things and people
- Some people will take advantage of you
- Can't ever let the bad people change you

PHILOSOPHY
- Give people the benefit of the doubt
- We're not going to kick you out if you make a mistake

ALW IS A TEAM
- Good coach, good team
- We learn lessons in this environment you can't learn anywhere else
- This team is a winner
- You are who you associate with
- You can't put yourself above the team
- You can't be a phony
- You need to be excited all the time whether you feel like it or not
- You have to have a hunger to get excited about our company
- I've never been happier with this company

- These great times will continue
- There will be happiness and fulfillment in this company from now on

POWER OF RECOGNITION
- You can't be great until you master recognition
- Recognize their strengths
- The only thing that keeps me going are the success stories in this company

WINNERS ARE ONLY LOOKING FOR OPPORTUNITY
- All they need is to see someone else like them making it
- If they can do it, you can do it
- It should give you confidence because someone else did it
- Winners seem to work out of fear. Scrambling all the time to find a way to win

There will be lots of doubts early in your career whether you are going to make it. Winners fight through that wall.

- You are this company to your people
- Leadership is everything. It's how you live your life.
- You can kill their dreams
- Believe this thing is good!

- We're not going to let you down
- There will be no disappointments here
- All ALW can do is give you an opportunity

- Get better every week. Be a positive influence on your people.
- People that love this company, believe in the real meaningful things in this company will win

I WANTED TO QUIT EVERYDAY
- Why do we do it? Because we want to Be Somebody.
- Keep pushing
- People will lay it on the line for you if you live your life for them and their families
- You receive the ultimate financial reward by helping other people
- There is a goodness and toughness in ALW
- We don't believe in the principles of ALW like Art does
- If you do these things your success will be phenomenal
- ALW was founded on the principles that made us unique

BASIC PRINCIPLE
- ALW is right 100% of the time
- The first step in being great is that you do something that is right. It is everything.
- We took confusion out of the life insurance and investment business

WE FOUND A BETTER WAY TO BUILD A COMPANY
- We found a better way to bring a better quality of person into the industry
- I've got to feel good about what I do for the consumer
- People need to see the goodness in the company
- This thing hasn't happened overnight. Thousands of people have come before you and laid it on the line.

- I've always wanted to Be Somebody
- I wondered whether I was tough enough… I found out I was
- ALW gave me an opportunity to get excited

- I feel like I was making a difference. People are better off because of me.
- There isn't anything else out there like ALW for people like me and you
- You've got to get the childlike excitement back in your life

- The business of winning is a serious business to me
- Attitude is everything

If people are thinking right, all they're looking for is an opportunity.

- This is nothing but a business of motivation
- Commitment comes with lots of pain and sacrifice
- Your people are an extension of you

- Our goal is to have all RVPs be a part of the Presidents Council
- All RVPs should do 30 sales or more a month in the base shop

TOP PRIORITIES
- Build friendships with your leaders
- Promote recruiting
- Your people have to believe you're right. They believe that you are an honest and sincere person.
- People like me want to believe in something, belong to something. They will fight and die for you if they do.

RECRUITING AND PRODUCING
- Recruit mad men and mad women that can get excited
- Prospect by recruiting
- Always talk about recruiting. Recruiting solves problems.
- Can't solve long range problems unless you recruit big numbers
- Promote cash flow: You must have somebody locally making money
- Promote competition
- Put the non producers on the bench
- Make heroes of the successful RVP's

RVP STANDARDS
- 15 sales per month - Poor
- 30 sales per month - Average
- 50 sales per month - Good
- 100 sales per month - Great

- Expect your people to win
- Desire to be recognized as a stud with your peers because it's a great compliment
- Never quit believing in your troops
- Be a personal example
- Be a winner. Do it first. Be a good person.
- Build strong personal relationships, which is a tradition in ALW

A KEY GOAL OF MINE
To live one day without a negative thought. If you're positive all the time, you'll win big.

TO WIN
The business has to become more than just a business. Leading people during good times and bad times

THE RVP POSITION
- Do it the ALW Way, not your way
- Make people feel special. Positive motivation Positive recognition. Give people responsibility.
- Raise good leaders like you raise good kids
- "No matter what you do, no matter how bad, I'll never quit loving you."
- Build it the ALW way
- All things ALW does, you should do
- Don't count on overrides until you are cash flowing $10,000 a month
- You have a responsibility to grow

- If you don't grow, you begin to die
- Increase recruiting. Increase sales
- Build more leaders. Build with quality. Recruit the right market. Sell the right market.
- Manage attitudes for growth with quality
- Freedom with responsibility
- We will deliver for the producers
- This is your opportunity to become stone wealthy
- Your organization is an extension of you
- Leaders live for the winners who stay and fight
- Your organization is an extension of you, your thinking, your ambitions, your visions, your desire

Work two or more levels below you as a way of life.

- You must be a crusader. Crusaders die hard.
- Be a crusader first and a businessman second

RVP - PARTNERSHIP IS A TEAM EFFORT BETWEEN SPOUSES
They have shared goals. They build relationships.

- Be totally loyal and committed to ALW and it's leadership philosophy.

I PROMISE
- The bubble will never burst
- You can expect miracles to happen

4/12/1984
HOUSTON, TX

GREAT LEADERSHIP
- Leaders are like a magnet. They are fun to be around and are dynamic.
- Great example in personal life
- Substance, quality, character about you

- Position does not make a person
- It takes 6 to 18 month to become an RVP
- 3 to 4 years of maturing process in ALW before it begins to fall in place for you
- Up until then it's a business of highs and lows

GO WIN! Only way to make all your problems and headaches worth it is to WIN.

HAVING PEOPLE PROBLEMS?
- You are the problem
- If I managed someone like you, I would get rid of you too
- To solve a problem, go out there and win
- Live for the good people
- Don't let negative people direct your life
- Management by intimidation is the easiest way to manage
- It takes guts to work with people, find their strengths and believe in them

MANAGEMENT
- Be a Crusader: understand the atmosphere you need is a dynamic and believing atmosphere
- People want to dream, they want someone to show them a way

GO AND BE
- The most enthusiastic
- The most dedicated
- Someone who believes in the dream the most
- We are dream sellers
- We give people new leases on life
- Our kind of people love it and want it
- Our job in ALW is to take a "have not" and show them, teach them, how to be a "have"

THERE ARE CHALLENGES THAT TRY TO KEEP YOU FROM WINNING
- Hard for you to keep trucking. It's an endurance contest.
- Fear of things happening to me that I have seen happen to other people
- Fear of losing personal endurance, personal toughness
- Do you have what it takes to do it again?
- Stay in the field: So you don't lose momentum
- You can't get away from doing the nasty things
- You are your best recruiter. No competition inside your company is a serious problem
- You stop working
- You get intimidated by the competition

TO WIN
- Develop the ability to live with the fact that you'll always be hurting and have enemies. Learn to live with it.
- Take a look at you and your business honestly
- Winners Attitude: to get better every day

- Look at your office. Is your office getting better? Just concentrate on that. Be getting better every week. Sometime later on you'll make it if you do.

ART ON LARRY WEIDEL: He struggled for 4 to 5 years. He was just getting by. But he just kept getting better.

WINNING IN MANAGEMENT IS LIKE COMPOUND INTEREST
- You work until the multiples get into place
- Do you have the courage to grind it out?
- The courage to keep building. To get a chance for the multiples to work for you
- There's a fine line. Work until you get to that fine line where your job is worth it
- You don't get a lot now. But you will!
- Now: make fortunes by recruiting and making sales from where you are
- How to make large numbers of sales? Recruiting large numbers of people.

TWO REASONS TO GET INTO MANAGEMENT
1. Override People
2. Build a Secure Income
    - No more mental anguish or fear of not making sales
    - Make a huge income
    - The top company producers get paid a lot of money

WE ARE A RECRUITING COMPANY
- Recruiting beats beating the bushes every day
- Sales is a lonely profession
- It solves your prospecting problem
- Everyone has a need to feel important. Insurance sales does not accomplish that
- It solves the turnover question
- People come and leave quickly in your normal sales company
- Sales people can't produce enough to make a big income
- "Big success legitimizes the opportunity."
- The best recruiting presentation is the asset management presentation with your paycheck
- To be as good as you can be you must be a 100% recruiter or 100% sales person
- Be a NUT about one thing: Recruiting
- A reason to get into recruiting is to prospect. It's a way to get more people and sales.

SPEAKER - ANGELA WILLIAMS

YOUR SPOUSE INVOLVEMENT IS NOT:
- Getting licensed or work in the business
- A Secretary for your husband
- To Have lots of meetings
- Money will only solve temporary partnership problems

Go do something out of the ordinary to show your spouse how much you love and appreciate them.

- Critical that the new recruit's spouse is reached early in this business.
- We spouses also have doubts about the future. The agent can make it but can we?
- It is mandatory that your partner know that they are making a contribution to the business
- You want to succeed in all areas of your life
- What you are as a person is important to us
- What an RVP can do for great spouse involvement: Work on relationships at home
- It all begins with you

Don't ever compare your partner to anyone else.

DON'T LET YOUR BUSINESS BE A THREAT TO YOUR MARRIAGE
- Ask your spouse to do things for you
- Find something for them to do. Read this book, listen to this tape
- Give your spouse partner a job that involves other spouses
- Call district manager spouses for you, be specific with instructions and keep it simple
- Change constantly to get them involved in many areas
- Spend time with the spouses in your organization
- They learn to respect you as a leader
- RVP must encourage spouse participation at the rep and manager levels

FACTORS
- There is no one way to do it. Dive in and do it. Be realistic.
- Have the right attitude. Don't quit
- Some will never catch fire
- Never lose your ambitions, goals, desires or the will to make the same commitment to the lives of other people

KEYS TO BUILDING
- Build two close personal friends in the business
- Have a plan, a purpose and announce it
- Learn to delegate
- Communicate on a regular basis
- Show your appreciation

6/8/1984
HAWAII HYATT REGENCY
MAUI, HI

- We've won! Everything is in place for us to win.
- Master the art of recognition, making your people feel special
- This Hawaii trip is a honeymoon and trip of a lifetime
- Develop a positive attitude about life
- Develop a positive, confident, excited, happy attitude

If you're down in the dumps, you've got an attitude problem... You've got an "I can't attitude."

WE WANTED ALW TO BE A COMPANY THAT DELIVERED FOR OUR FAMILIES
- Feel good about the permanency of what we have built
- ALW is a family
- If you can do an average job, you can build financial independence in a few years
- Our goals – to become one of the truly great businesses in this world
- We have to have a system everybody believes in
- We have got to produce leaders to make the system work
- We are positioned for greatness. It will take you along
- Build a company people will marvel at
- We've changed leaders in ALW. We are a confident, positive leadership team
- You don't think I love this company? I'm obsessed with it
- ALW is giving you a franchise and ready-made system
- We aren't changing the principles this company was built upon
- I want to win more than anything else in this world. But I want to win with class. I want the leaders of this company to be honest, and do good for others.
- A successful company can be judged by the leaders they develop
- We are building leadership for America
- We are proud of this leadership team at ALW

A LEADERS JOB
- Most decisions you make will turn out like you'd like for them to
- Make people feel good
- Recognize people doing special things
- We are Ambassadors of goodwill

3 THINGS
1. Create an atmosphere where people can be successful so our people can win
2. Master the art of recognition and making people feel good
3. Do it the ALW Way

2 THINGS CAN DESTROY THIS COMPANY
1. Hiring the wrong kind of people
2. Getting away from the principles and traditions we built this company upon, the goodness of ALW.

- Be a winner, make money, save money
- You have a chance to become wealthy and independent
- Never lose patience with your people

OUR THEME: I AM SOMEBODY

- I'm the kind of leader that plays scared. The game is never over
- Leadership is everything. We tried to be for real and honest with our people
- Our success legitimatized this opportunity.

- This opportunity is for real. We are delivering for people.
- The key to this business is being a crusader, and total commitment is everything. It gives you a sense of purpose, direction and contentment in your life
- A.L.Williams was built for the 2 percenters
- We've delivered for thousands of families

I want more than anything to have a company of integrity, honesty, sincerity. People have better lives because of this company.

TWO THINGS WE HAVE THAT WILL KEEP IT GOING ON FOREVER
1. A system everybody believes in
2. Leaders work the system in this unlimited opportunity
    - The real fortunes will be made 3 to 4 years from now

IT IS IMPORTANT TO WIN THE RIGHT WAY
- Being somebody is everything
- ALW is going to be known as the best company in American history
- ALW is built on the concept America was built upon. Freedom is the ultimate opportunity.
- We've created a special way to manage people
- Individual freedom and individual responsibility are our way of life in ALW
- Responsibility... Realize this really isn't your business. It is... and it isn't.
- To play on a team is a privilege, you represent everything you stand for. You affect the team. Don't put yourself above the team.

NATIONAL SALES DIRECTOR
- Build your hierarchy the ALW way
- Put your personality in it. Take the A.L.Williams system and compete, make a bunch of money
- Create and maintain an atmosphere of positive attitudes
- Maintain a competitive team attitude
- Guarantee, make the lowest level person in your hierarchy feel good
- Build successful leaders in this company
- How can I make my people more money
- I think of my people first
- We cleanse this company of people that would take advantage of people
- Be a personal, winning, positive example of that position. Be someone they can always count on.
- Leadership is the courage to get out and make it happen

WHY BE AN NSD?
- Highest level compensation
- Everybody wants to be an NSD
- Opportunity to make a difference in the lives of people
- Financial security for your family

NSD PERSONAL RESPONSIBILITY
- Always protect the company
- Don't put your personal interest above the team
- Never show fear
- Never show doubt
- Never show quit
- Call me anything but average and ordinary
- Call me anything but a mealy-mouth

THE DREAM
- To be a leader on a championship team
- For people to look at you and see greatness

WHAT MAKES ALW SPECIAL?
- For ALW to win we have to be heroes and leaders. Stand out from the crowd.
- I love this company, the people, what we stand for. If you like America, you've got to love ALW. ALW is proving the American dream is still alive.
- This is the only place in America that the American dream can come true
- The last 25 years, America has lost its competitive spirit
- America doesn't need protection. We need leadership. Where have all the leaders gone in America?
- The American people save less money than any other major country in the world
- America has programmed us. Telling us we're not good enough
- That college boards, grades, background, determine your success and your future
- People with average and ordinary backgrounds have to settle for that
- ALW was born believing that everybody wants to Be Somebody, wanting to build financial independence for their family
- The key is not education, but a will to win, to not be average and ordinary
- I believe that ALW is the future of America. Companies like us are turning around people's lives.
- This country was built on principles: Doing what's right
- We took a position in the industry to do what is right
- We build successful businesses by treating people right. We don't intimidate people.
- We deliver on our commitment
- We were built for a different kind of person
- We've built 40 to 50 financially independent people already and more to come
- This opportunity is better today than ever before
- ALW is a great company because it has a great heart
- You are rare and special and I love you
- ALW is in position to build millions of financially independent families

5 INGREDIENTS THAT MAKE OUR SYSTEM SO SPECIAL
1. Market: everybody needs our products and services
2. Products and our System: to serve the people who need us. We have no competition.
3. Recruiting: a paid referral system
4. Timing : perfect for today
5. Competitive Edge: our concept is right

8/12/1984

- I'm just a person that believes in winning
- Victory has to come before hard work pays off
- We've got to break records. You'll never be satisfied to just get by again.
- This is one hell of a company
- You win by building people
- We're going to have consistent growth for the next 2 to 3 years

RVP GROWTH TIPS
- Keep a contest going all the time
- Four day blitzes
- Recognition is the key to get people to work

Art Williams: Part 4

LEADERSHIP MEETINGS

1984-1985, 1988

ART WILLIAMS: PART 4
1984-1985, 1988

6/27/1984
CONFERENCE CALL

This opportunity is for real. We are in a moment of greatness. We're finished experimenting. We are confident. We are excited.

NSD - BUILD A COMPANY WITHIN A COMPANY
- Our goal is to have 50,000+ RVPs. One in every city and hamlet in America.
- A Company wins when the company can produce a national organization
- Who can take these services to America? It's going to be us
- NSD is the most important cog in the system. We need to put NSD's on a pedestal.

- You can't let negative quitters wear you out
- The leadership is in place to have this company go to greatness

WE'VE GOT TO GET MENTALLY TOUGHER
- We didn't have all we have today
- We had regulatory problems and we seemed to be tougher
- We built tough people that believe in our company
- 90 to 95% of the time people are not mentally and physically as tough as they need to be
- In the pros you don't do it with trick plays. We love it more than anybody else. We believe it more than anyone else.
- We need to challenge people to get tougher
- Standards of excellence means you strive for excellence
- Don't want to play on this team? Then get out!
- Get a mad on. Stir it up.

7/17/1984
NSD MEETING

PEOPLE HUNGER FOR OPPORTUNITY
- Attitude is the difference between being great and being average and ordinary
- All my business life I wanted to belong to something that is a cause and with people that I can win with
- It's a passion to me to build our company right, so that others can enjoy it

- To accomplish something that no one else in America can deliver for their people
- ALW is the unlimited dream and the unlimited opportunity
- It's giving me a reason to be optimistic, tough and positive
- I made up my mind when I arrived financially, that this is where I belong. Give other people the same opportunity that I had to prove something to themselves.
- At one time, my death would have torn this company up but not with our strength today
- The number one thing that can destroy our company is a lack of leadership
- We need strong, tough leadership to depend on
- We've got the strongest team in America. This thing truly is a dream come true.
- I hope you make up your mind to make a special contribution to your company and many, many people
- I hope you are creative for your family
- Everything we built has been built to make things better. That's not the kind of thinking in the industry and we will break some traditions.
- Winning is an attitude. If you're not winning you have an attitude problem that can be resolved by a decision to win.
- We've got everything in place to win. I hope you build a name for yourself.
- In the years to come you will realize that you really were very good
- Recognition is making people feel good and is the most important asset of a manager
- To make an impact, to be an NSD, you have to find a way to move armies of people
- You can't be scared and be a good head coach

MANAGEMENT PHILOSOPHY - HANDLING YOUR PEOPLE

- Talk about the positive things in people. Have a positive approach to management.
- Keep loving them
- No one decision is a bad decision
- It's the way you live your business life
- It's your overall attitude
- It's a pattern of thinking and decision making
- There's nothing black and white in management. There is no one way to win.
- It's the pattern of your showing up to work, having the courage to make a decision, and leading your organization to victory

- I'm tougher than anybody around this table
- Don't get too frustrated with things. The sun will come up.
- Be positive all the time
- Make a decision to get on with it

DECIDE TO WIN
- Go handle your people. You are an extension of the company.
- The company won't come back and second guess us
- I'm not going to agree with everything you do. That's the way it will be.
- Don't worry about making mistakes
- You must respect the company. You can't put yourself above the company or the team.

You can't tattoo and hurt a bunch of people! If you do, you deserve what happens to you.

- We run our own Hierarchy and the company and Art will leave us alone
- It's a privilege to play on this team
- You have to decide to win
- Leadership at times seems like you are the only one who cares or wants it
- The bigger you get in a company the less freedom you have

You build a huge HIERARCHY and a large number of people by being the RIGHT KIND of PERSON.

- We've given people the right to be an RVP. It is their business. They run it.
- They have freedom. We are a free enterprise company.
- People with freedom love it. The company protects the RVP's freedom.

- You must earn peoples respect
- You must prove that you are a good person to them
- Never say mine. You say "together we can do the impossible."
- You must work hard to earn peoples respect

Your primary job is a DREAM SELLER. You reinforce to them that this business will pay off for them and their families.

- Make people believe and have confidence that their families will win

- You've got to be excited about their families and their future

RVP is not a desk job. You be the hardest worker in your organization You LEAD, not manage, people into greatness.

ART'S PERSONAL PHILOSOPHY
- "I'm not the smartest, not the best, the only thing going for Art was that he was a plugger, and a fighter."
- You beat 50% of the people by working hard
- You beat 40% by being a good person, living right and finding something to believe in
- The last 10% is a dogfight
- Whatever you want your people to do, you go out and do it first

MANAGING YOUR PEOPLE
- Manage people the way you want to be managed
- The toughest management in the world is to get to know families

HOBBIES: I don't know anyone in this business that has a hobby.

What do you do to get this thing going? Just do SOMETHING and you will find out along the way what to do.

8/1/1984
NEW ORLEANS, LA
RVP MEETING

MY MINDSET
- I hope you can see a lot of confidence in me
- I had nightmares that maybe we would be disappointed one more time
- You need to get yourself in a position of total security
- I have no doubts and no fears that this is going to pay off for people
- We will win
- I'm a person that believes in winning
- I had dreams that one day I would be financially independent
- I wanted to quit 2 million times.
- But there was no chance to do anything big in any other opportunity
- I got up every day having to give myself a pep talk
- I'm totally positive every day. I build a positive attitude.

- The Most important asset in this company is being positive all the time
- In management you are either negative or positive. It's your choice.
- The role of a leader is looking at things in a positive way

You can't build a business quick...
The bigger things you go for take time.

- The role of a leader is to be positive
- It's vicious to go into business for yourself and become stone wealthy
- It's work only if you don't win
- If you don't win, the feelings you get will be deep with frustrations and life becomes a pain

I learned you've got to win. It's easier than the negatives of losing. To be pleased with myself I've got to win.

I don't like the work, the suffering, but I like the big override checks, the renewals, the feeling of winning.

- The reason we are here is called winning
- I went through anguish thinking some of our people wouldn't make it
- Keep showing up to work every day and you will win
- Just to think you can build financial independence and do something great for people along the way is incredible

- I love this company so much I can't stand it
- We've got to get positive
- Winning comes when you get competition going between reps in your base
- You better go through it
- You get no points until you hit the goal line
- The big meetings aren't what it's all about
- What you do in the next six months will determine what you do in your career

YOU ONLY HAVE TWO PROBLEMS
 1. Activity
 2. Attitude

- We are at a moment of greatness
- I really do believe our job is to push people up
- The role of a leader is looking at things positively

Go get something to be excited about when the crap is coming down around you.

- I have but one life to live
- I choose to be positive and live my life in a positive, optimistic manner
- Leadership to me is literally doing the impossible
- I promise you we will never slow down

Some believe there is an element of risk to continue to let it rip. I believe there is less risk by letting it rip.

- My promises is to keep this thing going so you can have your opportunity to make it big

I don't rank ALW the way other top people rank companies. ALW is a company of destiny.

- I just want to deliver for people
- To win with class and a lot of character. I believe in this strongly.
- You don't believe in 10% of what I do. You believe in 100%.
- I believe the only way we could continue to grow is to maintain the RVP position as an independent, free position. I fought to keep that position free.
- In order for you to accomplish the maximum, ALW has to give you your freedom

My greatest lesson as an assistant coach in high school: "You're the coach of the backs, you get them ready for Saturday night. Those are your backs." I took possession and ownership of my responsibilities.

FREEDOM
- I promise you your freedom
- You don't work for me or anyone else
- You are your own boss
- This is truly the American dream
- Freedom is the only way can we get to the maximum
- If I give you demands, you won't do it. You love it more and produce because of your freedom.
- You and you alone will determine your future

You can bet your butt that ALW will not disappoint you. But we will not wait for you either.

- The only way to keep this thing going is to train the trainer
- I'm betting the leaders will perform
- We grow in plateaus. You can't look at any one point in time and determine how your business is going. You are up one day down the next.
- You can't afford to get too high or too low. Avoid panic management.

START RECRUITING TODAY AND YOU WILL MAKE MONEY IN 90 DAYS
1. You can grow to new plateaus in 30 days if you really trust the system
    - Keep fighting every day. Don't get too comfortable.
2. Build 7 to 10 RVP's to become financially independent. You'll be stone wealthy.
    - Times are so special you can build 2 to 3 RVP's and you're on the road to being wealthy
    - You can accomplish things in 10%, 20%, 30% of the time than those of us who did it before you

- Now's the time to get it up. We are inside the 20 yard line.
- You can't wallow around. If you do you'll be a sad person.

Attitude is everything. The single greatest thing you can accomplish on his earth is to be excited, positive, confident, and have a great outlook about life.

I have fought all my life for success. All my life I wanted to do what meant something to me. Everything worthwhile is nasty to get. There isn't any easy way.

This business won't work if you don't lay it all on the line to the point where people think you are stupid

- You must be willing to do it long enough
- Everything I did that was worthwhile and meaningful was worth it
- The biggest surprise you'll have is that you can perform average and become wealthy here
- A good RVP is doing 15 to 20 sales a month

Show me a person who wants to go into this business and become a successful RVP in six months and they will.

The toughest management principle is not letting the disappointments and the negative people change you.

DON'T THINK THAT EVERYONE OUGHT TO MAKE IT
- The numbers will never change
- 98% of the people are not willing to pay the price
- As a leader you have to live for the 2% who are STUDS
- It's easy to quit
- Live for those who stay and fight
- ALW has delivered for you

TO WIN
- Be a winning example
- Do it the ALW way
- Don't hurt your team
- We've got to make this thing work
- Bring the crusading aspect back to ALW
- In order to win you must get fundamentally sound. 90% of the time you are not tough enough, mentally, fundamentally, and physically
- It's how tough they are and how much they believe in it that causes them to win
- People don't believe in it enough and don't love it enough
- I look at everybody as an RVP and treat them the same as an RVP

A Recruiting interview should last five hours over 4-5 meetings.

- I don't work with an RVP today that I don't believe wants to become stone wealthy
- It's a privilege to wear the RVP uniform
- This Team is not built for half butts
- If you're struggling, I've been there
- As long as your people believe right, you'll be a leader in this company

"As long as I'm with you, you make me feel like I've got a chance to win."... This is what your team should think.

WE WON BECAUSE...
- We had pride
- We were Crusaders to the core
- We believed we were different
- We believed we would win

- Thousands had dropped out thinking we were crazy

- If you're good enough to be on this management team, you going to be proud
- Don't you dare lay down in the fourth quarter. It's nauseous to me

I don't think it's sad to sacrifice, to do without, to struggle; if you win, it's all worthwhile.

- I'm talking about your life, your family
- A.L.Williams is no job, it isn't worth it if it's just a job
- I expect an RVP to be wealthy, to be excellent

WE WANT TO WIN A CHAMPIONSHIP
- Don't ever let me think that you are content to just get by
- If you don't want to win I don't want you on this team
- It is important to be striving to get there
- You never really accomplish your goals because you keep raising them
- Go Be Somebody great in America

RECOGNITION
- You can never recognize people too much
- Find creative ways to recognize people
- Foster an atmosphere in your organization of being positive

DO IT THE ALW WAY
Be an outstanding leader. Lead by personal example. Your people will copy you.

ALW is not built for superstars. It is built for people that are scared to death, that have no confidence, that fear sales, that don't think they can make big money.

When I recruit I talk to people like I would like people to talk to me. I can relate to people who screw up, that are scared to death, that have never sold anything, and still want to make it.

TIME IS EVERYTHING
- The reason for failure is that people don't give it enough time
- No one makes it with a hobby
- You can't skip steps
- This is a numbers business

BE TOUGH: You've got to be tough. You can't be a pansy and win. Once you are a crusader, it gives you the extra ounce of courage it takes to win.

LEADERSHIP IS EVERYTHING
- People will or won't follow you
- I'm serious about this moment. I've seen enough struggle, enough heartache.
- Winners win and losers lose
- You can't phony it up in the big leagues
- I believe in making it
- To win you need to do ugly things every day
- To make your family proud of you must win
- You only have one life. Decide to win and win big in that life.
- Sell the dream

ART'S PROFILE OF WINNING AND LEADERSHIP
1. People buy you, not the concept or opportunity, but because of your 100% total commitment
2. Recruit people with the crusade, with what we do for people, what we do for our team and what we do for our opportunity
3. Art had a vision of a national distribution system
4. Art never would tell you there was any chance you could fail
5. Art never asked how many sales you made, or how much premium you did. He always asked how many good people you recruited
6. The only control you have is activity and attitude
7. The first step to greatness is having a 100% commitment. A commitment to the big time, to the compensation system to yourself and then you will be successful.
8. People can spot a phony a mile away
9. Believe it will happen to you or you won't recruit anyone
10. I want to be known as a person that hires the most losers. In doing that Art had the most winners.
11. No one looks after your future better than you

- Art is consumed with winning. Winning for your people is all that there is.
- Believe in your winning destiny. You were born to win
- Turn all your negatives into positives
- You have to be a rock for your organization

- They look to you for strength, vision, and leadership
- Don't get confused with a prestigious position and opportunity
- Loyalty is important to Art Williams

- Art Williams makes people feel good
- Art builds a special kind of loyalty with his people. They are in this thing with him to the end.

- Would your people choose you to get into a foxhole with them? How do your people really see you?
- Do you always look out for yourself first? Art always looked out for his people first.
- Art is more motivated now than ever. He gets a thrill by watching people grow.

- Art is motivated by the competition. He is a totally fierce competitor.
- Art got after the competition
- When you get down, get after them

I BELIEVE
1. Those that are failing in ALW have a prosperity problem
2. Not making money? You have prosperity problem by not telling the story to enough people.
3. Anyone who made it big must master the referral and recruiting prospecting system of ALW
4. This is a numbers business. The more recruits the more probability of success.
5. What do you do with the new recruit is just as important as recruiting the huge numbers
6. Recruiting and selling… you must do both

WHAT IS ALW?
ALW is NOT a mass marketing organization. There are weaknesses in mass marketing…
- They give a bad impression
- They ruin your name and reputation
- They saturate your name
- They blow prospects natural markets
- Mass marketers don't have time to build personal relationships
- Mass marketing is not effective

You can't win long range by cold calling, running ads, flyers, and knocking on doors. Our uniqueness is that we built a recruiting management concept in sales.

FUNDAMENTALS OF RECRUITING AND PROSPECTING
- Prospect by recruiting
- 10 people talk about buying something, nine get turned off
- Don't over-promote the opportunity
- SELL part time aspect. SELL no risk
- Spend the necessary time to do it right
- Do not bring a recruit to an opportunity meeting without first selling the concept
- A new recruit sale should be done in three step process
- Protect a new recruits natural market
- We've solved the prospecting problem
- Field training sales are mandatory
- Recruit ALW type of people. Professional sales people have screwed up their natural markets
- Create a fantastic sense of urgency
- Recruit the selective masses
- Recruit all the time
- The best recruiting presentation is the asset management presentation. That's our uniqueness.
- A happy client is the best prospect to recruit
- Master the art of referrals. When things go down, double or triple your activity.
- Recruit by day sell by night
- Recruit every client

GOALS FOR NIGHT TIME ACTIVITY
- Have an average of four nights a week at the kitchen table
- Average two presentations per night
- The best way to prospect during the day is to prospect with recruits natural market
- Have a recruit take the day off, half-day off, and have lunch appointments with them
- Build and maintain, all the time, a good prospect list
- Keep a list of your clients
- Goal? Recruit 50% of your clients

It might take you 3 to 4 times to recruit someone who is special.

- Write a list of all people that bomb out of other businesses, who got their nose bloody and quit, but are a good person
- Be aware of what's happening in your daily life: PTA, school, just meeting people
- Face to face recruiting

- Keep planting seeds that will pay off 60 to 90 days from now

- Cold calling should only be done if you have no natural market and it should only be done for a short period of time
- Always ask a question: "Have you ever heard of ALW? Have you ever seen the book Common Sense?"
- Pick up business cards

- Lists: New homeowners. Babies. Clubs. Church. PTA. Teachers. Coaches. Sales people.
- "STEAM" your current people and clients
- Very marginal method: Newspaper ads

The way to prospect is through a new recruits natural market.

8/14/1984
NSD MEETING

SPEAKER - ANGELA WILLIAMS

- Help our spouses feel good about what they are doing
- Our lives are fragmented. We need to help our partners find their role.
- Each person has a different talent
- Motivate and pull out your partners strengths

SPEAKER - ART WILLIAMS

- The mental pressures are greater than the physical pressures

Building an organization is better than any stock market investment you can make.

- We're going to make millions
- I'm proud of you. I love this business.
- You can't let negative people tear you down. You can't let 2% of the people make you negative. 98% of the people are positive.

- People can't be honest with themselves. They B.S. themselves.
- Everybody believes they paid a bigger price than anyone else
- The more you do for people the more you leave yourself open for Criticism

- People can't see themselves the way an unbiased, unprejudiced person can see them
- The goal is helping people become better people

APPRECIATE
- The complexity of our business
- Our way of management is the toughest kind of management in the world
- I want to run this company as a family

NSD POSITION
- Everybody has feelings of frustration and guilt
- It's hard for me to relax and take time off. We have to learn how to deal with it. It's lonely at the top.
- Pass positives down and negatives up and understand you have no one to share it with.
- The feeling that what you're doing is not worth anything is tough and normal
- You have lots of difficult choices that occupy your time and make you second guess yourself that what we do is right. So fight the thought to not do anything at all.
- Art believes in the Peter principle (Performance based promotions)
- Everybody hits their level of incompetence
- Leaders seem like they've got the pulse of their organization and can do what is needed for their organization
- Art Williams believes that changing things is the only way to grow. You can't get too organized, if you do you won't grow.

10/23/1984
NSD MEETING
STONE MOUNTAIN, GA

- Our top responsibility is to communicate with our people
- You can do in 3 to 4 years what we did in 10 to 12 years
- Our job is to motivate our people. Make people feel special
- Attitude is everything
- ALW was built for sales people and run by sales people
- No one will run this company without a sales background. Nothing else works.

In 1977 we said we were going to take all the B.S. out of a corporation. Everyone has a chance if they can produce. It's a way of life in ALW.

- You have to be a company of principles to win
- Try to live right and honor your reputation
- If we are good enough to build this thing, we are good enough to run it

It seems that we built our team with people that no one else had a lot of desire for. People who had desire but not a great resume.

- Only in America. Only here can a guy like me start part time, with no chance, and become a millionaire.
- ALW represents America and all this country believes in
- ALW allows you freedom to run your own business
- We ask people to do the impossible
- Art is a madman, every great person wants to Be Somebody!
- Winning and making people proud of you - your family, friends, and people you respect - that's what life is all about
- ALW gives me a chance to be a stud, to always grow, to excel

YOUR TOP PRIORITIES
- Motivation – Sell the DREAM
- Push people up. It has to be a way of life. We make people feel special.
- 95% of the plays you call don't work. Just keep calling the shots.
- If your heart is in the right place, you will win
- Growth - either you are growing or you are dying
- I want to win the World Series and the Super Bowl every year
- Be the right kind of example: of integrity, of character
- I'm the only person I can count on 100% of the time
- When you muster the courage to go out and do it, they will follow you.
- Courage must be a way of life
- You can't demand love from people
- Loyalty and respect doesn't come without displaying courage
- You be the hardest worker. You make the most money.

KEY TO GREATNESS
- Key to greatness? You work for your people
- People in the field love us when things are going good
- I've got to keep working to keep things going. I live for the people in ALW.
- I want ALW to stand for something.

Success is not one big victory, but thousands of little victories.

- What you do as a head coach is a statement about your life
- Winners: You can't worry about making mistakes
- At this level you've got to perform. Don't try to protect the lead.

WE ARE ON THE THRESHOLD OF DOING SOMETHING GREAT
- How many shots do you have at doing something great?
- People are waiting in the wings to beat our butts
- We can't ever do enough, can't make enough, can't RECRUIT enough, can't save enough money, can't make enough money.
- The day you're not driven like you should be, you should step down from the job
- You've been chosen, you are living the dream
- But the position doesn't make a person
- Just keep making decisions day to day. Keep trying to win.
- Winning must become a way of life. Think it, live it and do the things to win.
- You must grow to become an NSD

*"Art **CHEWED** us out at this meeting." Bill Orender*

The Peter Principle: You can never outgrow and max out. You can always grow if it's in your heart. It's how you feel about yourself.

IF YOU ARE A SELF CENTERED PERSON IT IS IMPOSSIBLE TO CONTINUE
- Life saps your energy, enthusiasm and strength because you're always thinking about yourself
- Worries beat you down so you can't succeed
- Giving principle. The bigger the executive the more you've got to give as a person
- Only way to grow is to give to other people
- They in turn give back to you
- Attitude, will to win, enthusiasm
- The more people you help, the more you get because they give back to you
- You can't do things only because it will make you more money.
- Dedicate your life to your people and appreciate yourself
- Get rid of all the jealousy, greed, envy, take your life and give it to your people
- When you win, give all the credit to your managers. When you lose, take all the blame.
- Be patient because people grow in plateaus

10/24/1984

- The position doesn't make the person, the person makes the position
- It's impossible for good people to get lost in our company
- Either you are or you are not financially independent. Either you are or you aren't somebody.

- If we're good enough to build it we're good enough to run it

- We are free enterprisers to the core
- Unlimited freedom. Unlimited responsibility.
- We use the resources of ALW

- Managers work for their people. Their people don't work for the manager.
- Most times business principles are in conflict with people principles

Crusading spirit. The Crusade is not good without the opportunity. The crusade is in vain without an opportunity.

I BELIEVE IN WINNING
- Everyone I know who wins is a madman
- Don't deny me my right to be a madman. To work hard, to decide not to be average and ordinary, not to be a half butt, just because you choose to be average and ordinary

CORNERSTONES OF ALW
- We believe everybody wants to Be Somebody
- To win you have to learn how to compete
- Life will give you whatever you will fight for
- Everybody wants to win and succeed, but most don't want it bad enough
- Happy or sad, you have to fight for those things that you want
- Dream of excellence and have a goal of being somebody
- Have a big dream, with little victories along the way

TWO DECISIONS
1. Believe in something and have goals for it. Otherwise you are doing without and screwing around. You have to work hard without something to believe in. You'll be miserable and frustrated.
2. Decide the price you will pay. Loyalty, work hard, having something you can believe in, winning, building, Your family will be proud of you, your children will be proud of you.

BUILD A LARGE ORGANIZATION
- Do what's right. Your reputation is everything.
- Stand for something
- I try and motivate people with a cause. Freedom is a cause; financial independence is a cause.
- We stand for something. We do what's right for the consumer.
- The key to winning is to be tough but be a good person

- Factor the human factor in every management decision
- No rules - guidelines are the best things to have in a company

"ALMOST" IS A WAY OF LIFE FOR MOST PEOPLE
- Most people almost WIN
- Most people almost try
- Most people almost succeed
- "Almost" has become a way of life for most people

- Be tough, win, be good, have integrity
- A leader is the hardest worker, the best recruiter. They do everything they are supposed to do and then they do a little bit more.
- A leader thinks about their business all the time
- Praise and recognition are the cornerstones of building
- Give, give, give and expect nothing in return

Recognition, without praise, is no good.

- The ultimate form of leadership is doing first what you ask your people to do
- You've got to be what you want your people to be
- Eyeball to eyeball management is the best kind of management
- I love selling, I love recruiting

- Winning is an attitude
- Motivation is everything
- I want to talk about your life, your winning and the DREAM
- If people believe they can win, how good will it be when they do win

- Recruit and sell and all the rest will fall into place
- Nothing in my life that ever meant anything came easy
- ALW was born to inspire you to improve your life. It was not to improve products but to improve your life. If $200 a month will improve your life, we are improving your life.

10/19/1984

Sacrifice early to have later, or have now and sacrifice forever.

ART'S MINDSET
- I want to Be Somebody
- Sacrifice to win. I've got to live with myself if I don't do it.
- It's me, my record, my vision, my hard work, my dedication that I have to live with for the rest of my life. What I did and didn't do.

ART'S VIEW OF LIVING
- We have a destiny. We are changing an industry. We are making a difference
- People are counting on us. I resent people who think that dedication and purpose is being a workaholic and indicates that we don't care about our families. Theirs is really an attitude of condemnation of how I've chosen to live my life.

TO BE A WINNER
- Keep your mind on the things that you want and off the things that you don't want
- Talk success, not failure
- Are you willing to pay the price?
- Write down your goals. Review your written goals for 30 minutes each day and let the ideas flash into your mind.
- Picture yourself already in possession of what you want
- Try to recognize, relate, assimilate and apply principles you hear
- Memorize quotations that will inspire you
- Learn how to help yourself, by sharing your knowledge with others
- Memorize the self starter: "Do It "

WINNING CAN BE LONELY
- People tell you not to work so hard
- Your spouse tells you not to work so hard
- Assistant coaches tell you not to work so hard…Yet the head coach is the one who has to live with the scoreboard. It's a total reflection on him. Reflection on his decision, commitment, vision, reason for being, his effort, his self-esteem.

I RESENT
- I resent someone else trying to place their values on me
- I resent average and ordinary people ridiculing my ambitions
- I resent those whose dreams are small and who ridicule me and put my vision down and say I'm a workaholic and I don't care about my family
- I resent those who are self righteous, who look down at me, who shrug their shoulders, who shake their heads, let out a little disgustful laugh and ridicule my desire, ridicule my ambitions, ridicule my goals, and ridicule my destiny

- Maybe you can't understand why I work like I work, why my fanaticism, because you don't understand my reason for being, my destiny, why I was put on this earth
- Don't impose your beliefs on me, don't insinuate I don't love my family, or my God, or life, because I have a vision
- I am not sure whether I could live with myself if I don't accomplish my dreams

WINNING TO ME IS
Working hard, dreaming big, dedicating your life to something and then having to fight friends, family, and the lost souls who ridicule your desires.

ATTITUDE
- Attitude is our number one job
- It is a requirement to succeed, along with being positive, being excited and being enthusiastic
- Know that this is a forever, lifetime position. That you're not going anywhere. That this is your last job.
- That is being positive and excited
- You're going to screw up, just regroup and plan to get better
- Be positive and believe it will get better. If you don't believe it will get better, you have an attitude problem.

Recruiting and premium are the result of doing things right on the front end.

SPOUSE
Your spouse is the most important person in your hierarchy;
Tell her every day.

RECRUITING
- Recruit large numbers
- Keep your priorities straight

Recruiting is an endurance contest.

THINK OF WHAT YOUR ALTERNATIVE IS....
- If not ALW, what?
- If not now, when?
- If not you, who will make the difference? WHO?
- Be a crusader. Crusaders die hard. A CRUSADE looks like a job that isn't a job. It's a chance to believe in something. It's a chance to Be Somebody
- Decide to do it and get it over with

- Decide to be financially independent. Winning means building total financial independence for your family.
- Have a goal of greatness in your life
- Expect a miracle

12/9/1984
"WE BEAT PRU" CELEBRATION
BOCA RATON, FL

- ALW built to give people like me a chance to Be Somebody
- The chance to be among the best
- We did something people said couldn't be done. We have a chance to dominate this industry forever.
- This company is formed from people who are fed up with corporate America
- Our model? Sales people are king
- Success for our families is why we are here
- All my life I've wanted to Be Somebody
- I want to deliver for your families to become financially independent
- I want you to make real money and save your money

MY PROUDEST MOMENT IN THE INDUSTRY
- When I made my first sale in this business
- When I went full-time and I was scared for two years
- When I paid my first death claim
- When I had my first old agent and confrontation
- When I was paid $100,000 in one year
- When I took my first airplane ride with this company
- When I founded ALW in 1977
- When I had my first RVP promotion
- When the first ALW person was paid $100,000
- When we opened our home office
- When we broke $1 billion in production in one year
- When we had our first convention here in Boca Raton
- When we took our first company trip to Europe
- When we broke ground on our very own home office
- When American Can company bought us out
- When I wrote the book *Common Sense*
- When we hit $3 million in compensation our first year
- When the Saturday Evening Post article came out about ALW
- When I became financially independent
- When we produced 75 cash millionaires in our first seven years in business
- When we came out with the Wall of Fame

- When we promoted the first NSD, now we have 22
- When we started to produce a $100,000 earner each month
- When we had the first person paid $1 million in one year
- When we came out with the $100,000 club, and gave out $100,000 rings
- ***But our proudest moment was beating Prudential in 1984.***

- We can't let fear keep us from being great. I want you to Be Somebody you are proud of.
- ALW was found for people like you to have a chance to do something great
- Our number one goal is to give you and your family a chance to become financially independent and stone wealthy.

DO...
- Spend time every day dreaming
- See yourself doing something great
- Read biographies of your heroes
- Be proud and love the things this company stands for and get emotional about building your own company
- Start competing
- Be a powerful, winning, personal example that people want to be around
- Give yourself a checkup. Decide what you need to improve upon
- Become a powerful example to your people that you come in contact with

12/12/1984
BOCA RATON, FL

Have the attitude that everybody you recruit is a future superstar. I look at everybody as an RVP.

- Build depth in a relationship
- Winners are Crusaders first
- ALW was born for a different kind of person. If you fail, it's because you didn't want it bad enough.
- Everybody is important in ALW, everybody is necessary
- As a leader you work for your people
- Push up people and make people feel proud

A new recruit needs to understand the crusade and the dream.

- See yourself winning and being somebody that you are proud of

- I want to serve you. If you win, I win. If you lose, I lose.

12/15/1984
BOCA RATON, FL

- We have a chance few Americans have a chance to get. We have a chance at greatness.
- Our challenge is to build leaders and put them in leadership
- My job is to build a company within a company. It's one company but you can build it 22 different ways.
- All I ask is your loyalty… Handle the competition right
- Don't compare yourself to each other - You can't tell who's really winning for a few years.

Winning is 80% to 90% enthusiasm, excitement and motivation.

FEEL GOOD ABOUT YOU
- You have to make yourself feel good about you
- We all doubt, we all feel insecure, we all feel inadequate
- Our ability to deal with these human emotions determines whether or not you're a stud
- Grow to Be Somebody that you are proud of

PRIDE
- I can leave a legacy of greatness and make a contribution to this movement or I take the money and run. Take the money and run and you will be a bitter old man
- Get all areas of your life in order
- We have a chance to make a major contribution and the money will be a byproduct of that.

In order to become a great leader, you have to become a great person first.

Being somebody and doing something with your life and something that you are proud of and having a reason to get up in the morning is important.

- The dream job in America has to be a leader in ALW
- **We are the National Champions!**

3/12/1985

Every time you have a meeting, do something more spectacular than the time before

- I promise you I will deliver for you and your family
- I'll never disappoint a producer and a leader

6/6/1985
ACAPULCO, MEXICO

- I have such feelings of pride that I swell up inside

Everybody had the same feeling that you have, they want to quit or commit suicide. But with the top leaders that feeling doesn't last long.

All you can do is all you can do and all you can do is enough

- Who is counting on us? Our families and the people we promised to succeed with.
- I'm so proud of being a part of this company and of this team

Feel good about yourself. And the only way to feel good about yourself is by making a contribution.

- The motivation has got to come from within. Real and sincere motivation.
- Be a master motivator. Motivate yourself first.
- Stir it up. Be creative.

When you slow down, question what that something is that is telling you to slow down.

- When you're moving as an army it may take you years to move
- Moving a platoon you can move that in a day. ALW is a monstrous army.

You can't make a mistake as a leader if you follow your instincts. Keep working, keep hustling, keep charging, follow your instincts and you'll become what you want.

It's hard, vicious work to build a base shop.

- I am a worker. I love to work when I work. But I don't always like it. Just be a worker, a madman.
- You will find your uniqueness and do your thing
- You make your system go because you're excited about your system
- You can't make a mistake if you believe in your heart that you are right

- Be flexible. You can't do anything more than 3 to 5 months and then you got to change.
- Keep going. Get on a roll. Run a mature organization and in 18 months you'll be a seasoned RVP.
- Go for the most quality first generations as you can
- Do you feel that you're doing a good job?

A SURGE is moving your organization. To get a surge all you need is 1 to 2 more studs. A SURGE can push you 23 years forward.

- I've got to have leaders around me that feel good about our company, themselves, me and our system. There's nothing that can ever split us apart or to cause me to doubt you.

WHAT TO DO
1. BE HAPPY.....
    - You motivate you. Don't wait on me to motivate you. Create a position of responsibility.
    - Make a contribution where you feel good about you. We have a chance to make mega-money.
2. GROW…Compare yourself now to where you were one year ago.
3. BE A POSITIVE EXAMPLE for your people. I'm happy with you if you do these things.
    - I'm happy to be in business with you. People are counting on you and me to lead, not to quit, not to feel sorry for ourselves.

6/7/1985
ACAPULCO, MEXICO

This is not a game to me. This is serious business.
We are going to be really big.

YOU NEED TO BE STRONG IN 6 AREAS
1. Be ready and capable of handling the competition
2. Market; The market will ultimately determine your success in business. It is impossible to recruit or sell enough people.
3. Our delivery system is unique and is championing the cause of part-timers. We found a better way to build a company.
4. Money availability; We signed a contract with a huge coalition of big banks
5. Administration capabilities
6. Quality of business. Quality of people determine your quality of business because of the quality of people you recruit will ultimately determine your success.

The person that will determine whether or not you succeed is you. You've got to bring a burning desire, a discipline, sacrifice, and be the right kind of person.

Go out and compete, fight and work hard. How hard will you fight to be financially independent and to be financially free? Would you be willing to do the nasty things to be financially independent? Are you willing to Recruit, build , build a base shop, make money and save money?

Why do winners win? They win because of desire and determination. You've got to create inside of you a fantastic desire that sticks with you. If you ever lose it, you're dead.

QUALITIES OF AN NSD
- They play scared and have a knot in their stomach
- They wake up scared every morning
- They are nuts. They can't be satisfied with the money they're making. This is constructive discontent.
- They are driven people. They want to be recognized as special and as a stud
- They do whatever it takes to win. They do it first and work the hardest
- They are hungry. They want recognition.
- They are mad men. They are eaten up with it.
- They are never satisfied and always have another mountain to climb
- They are possessed and their motors are always running

- They care deeply about people, their families and getting their people financially independent
- They know they were put on this earth to Be Somebody
- They are confident people. They analyze their weaknesses and turn them into strengths.
- They look for positive things in people
- They are always positive
- They have a cause and something to get mad at
- They smell success and see themselves winning
- They have fabulous instincts caused by desire
- They are eaten up on the inside
- They are a possessed person
- They have a goal of greatness and a desire to be financially independent

We need to manage with a 100% commitment. Like marriage, there is no 50/50 commitment.

- Learn to compete within yourself. Outside and inside competition can't slow you down.
- I know attitude is everything
- There is a 90% chance of financial independence if you're excited and positive
- I am positive that you can and will win

UNDERSTAND HUMAN NATURE
- Life can be a pain in the butt or it can be a wonderful, beautiful experience.
- Attitude is everything
- Every single day I worry. I doubt. I want to go out and get a good job. I think maybe I should quit and be like everybody else. But I only feel like that for 45 seconds and then I go on. I overcome my negative feelings with my positive attitude.
- What's inside of you will determine your desire, no matter how many negative thoughts bombard you. Don't you let those things destroy you.

The difference between a $20,000 and $100,000 person is how they feel about what they do. Get excited about this thing!

- If you could make it to Acapulco maybe you can make it to financial independence

8/16/1985

- The purpose of any organization is to get results
- Showing up is 80% of A.L. Williams
- Manage your business as a people business not an insurance or sales business
- Constantly be selling the dream
- The bigger you are the more genuine you must become

GAINING MOMENTUM - MAKE A BIG PLAY
- In every football game there are various BIG PLAYS that can turn the momentum around in your favor. An interception, fumble recovery etc.
- You have got to make the big play. You go out and recruit one direct a week and do $2,500 a week personally
- You go out and become the "Bell Cow" of your organization and make the big play

6/20/1988

- Why am I a winner? Because I'm a crusader
- Some of you have a pansy attitude. The enemy can't win.

- Mega wealthy: Not everybody but just a few want to be mega wealthy
- Not everybody who is an RVP, just a few, want to be wealthy
- You fight every day in every way

- Am I going to suck it up and go back to teaching or am I going to stay and fight?
- How long can you fight the fight?
- How much do you believe in the crusade?

1985

A.L. WILLIAMS WAS FORMED TO
- Give people like me and you a chance of financial independence
- Give people a chance for a new, prosperous life
- To build security for us and our families
- To hope that it will get better
- To live the kind of lives we want to live
- To do something special with our lives
- For a chance to Be Somebody

THE ALW MOTTO
"We the willing, led by the unknown, are doing the impossible for the ungrateful. We have done so much, for so long, with so little, we are now qualified to do anything with nothing."

BOE ADAMS
- Time for us to go for it. Let it fly.
- Stop being conservative. Be aggressive.
- This is a special time

ART WILLIAMS
- Why do you love it and why do those who quit not love it?
- Quitters are just lazy individuals
- We see ourselves involved in a larger role than just our businesses
- Character, all the winners have character
- When you hit a wall, just don't quit
- We are part of something unique in American business
- You'll never be denied your opportunity to be in business and be as big as you want to be here
- The greatest thrill is to see lives changed
- The courage some of our people display is incredible
- I'm proud to see people grow and feel good about themselves
- It's tough to stay up, tough to stay believing, tough to keep it going

Is it possible to work at ALW and not make it, even though you try? No!

You need to possess that belief, that child-like commitment.

- The mental aspect is everything. You must believe. Believe you actually will find a way to win.
- Just go out and do it
- Work on your mindset and attitude. That's what this is all about.
- Do you ever doubt it will ever pay off? I do not believe you can be an RVP, pay the price, and not make it.

- Takes time – People quit too soon before they get it going
- If you really pay the price you will win

Those that are making it cry together.

- You can't make a dud into a stud

- People make you believe they're totally committed. When the real story comes out they really aren't.
- It's hard for most people to be honest with themselves
- We will never fail you
- If you blow ALW, it means you weren't ready for it

You don't believe like I believe, you don't want it like I wanted it.

- I know in my heart it will pay off
- A big opportunity has a big price. The only thing I could count on is me busting my butt; investing myself into my business.
- I really don't like what we have to do to get the job done, of getting no's, of working nights, but I like the results.

- The best way to manage is by instincts
- You must be willing to change
- Don't let things destroy your confidence
- You can't keep riding the same horses. Go get new ones.

Create controversy even if things are going good.

- I want to build this company as a family
- Lead your people during the tough times
- Can we retire? Yes. But how could we live with overrides with people counting on you?
- We've chosen an uncommon life

- The insecurity and the pressures were frustrating. But we couldn't have any other kind of life.
- We are a different kind of people
- Together we are one awesome force in the industry

Art Williams: Part 5
POSITIVE WINNING ATTITUDE
1984-1985

ART WILLIAMS: PART 5

7/1/1984

FINANCIAL DIGNITY
- Our goal is to bring to millions of Americans financial dignity
- We are at war with being broke, with having to do without, with families telling their children "we can't afford it"
- Our company is here to renew a dream in the hearts and minds of Americans that they in- fact can dream again, realize it's going to get better, and the dream that having a life on credit and regret is not necessary.

FALSE SECURITY, FALSE DREAMS
- People at my former job give 10–20 years of their life, betting on the future. They do the things that their friends, family, educators and society said would bring them success, security and pride. Now they are either shelved or out of jobs due to mergers and acquisitions.
- They gave 20 years of dreaming, hoping, believing in a false dream. The dream of corporate America is dead.
- Corporations know that the dream they sell to people of getting promotions, of success, power, of triumph is a lie when they tell it.
- We are giving a new vision, a new dream to America, the dream that is not a lie, not based on if things go well, or if you are a fair-haired person.
- Position of success should be based on individual desire not what's available
- We alone in America are providing total security for families, security that is not found on or depending upon what a company is doing today.

THERE IS NO HOPE WITHOUT ALW
- Realize it's over out there in the corporate world
- What magical thing is coming your way through corporate America, a school system, or whatever organization you were working for that will make a difference?
- The average white collar pay raise in 1983 was 3.7%. The traditional American dream that is perpetrated on the middle class is a lie.
- For decades people have been believing it, where has it gotten them? Further mired in mediocrity and hopelessness....
- Social Security is a mess, retirement that will only pay one-half of what is promised

- It's about realizing that you have to do something. No trust fund daddy is watching over you. You are not a chosen person.
- But ALW are the chosen people. Chosen to bring financial independence, dignity, self respect and restore lives destroyed by financial pressures.
- I truly believe we are the resurrection of the American dream. We alone are the hope of millions of Americans.
- I was so tired of being broke, so tired of doing without, of telling my family no, of telling my wife to cut back, of lying to myself that I was doing better than I was, that my financial situation wasn't as bad, of being paid a cost of living increase.
- I was crying inside with the financial frustrations I had and finally, I all but gave up.

OUR PLAN
- To bring this opportunity to our people, our kind, people like us, people with families like ours, with fears like ours, with frustrations like ours
- If they've got a dream left, if they have the slightest ambition, we will show them the financial promised land

I'VE GOT A DREAM
- The dream of financial security and independence that we have in America of new homes, cars, education for children, financial peace of mind, financial security and a new and wonderful financial self-respect and pride for our people.
- The dream of family happiness with financial freedom. Children not being brainwashed, looking at money as a pain.

HOW DO YOU FEEL ABOUT THIS SYSTEM
- It was for me and my family and an enormous number of other families and their personal financial improvement that we were born
- It was our chance to Be Somebody, to let us see how good we are, to provide an opportunity to grow and build at our speed

MONEY
- Money becomes a god when you think about it all the time, when you don't have it
- How many times a day does the lack of money come into your mind?
- Money for food, clothes, dental bills, gasoline, bills in the mail, writing checks, credit cards not for convenience, but for a lack of having money.

7/12/1984

ALW - A NEW KIND OF HEROISM
- People reaching down to come up with the energy to make their life something special
- A kind of heroism that is void in America today
- ALW allows a person to justify their existence

LOVE PEOPLE ENOUGH TO HELP THEM
- Build people to Be Somebody that they are proud of
- Push them up to new promotion levels
- The pride that comes with achievement
- The inner reward of setting and accomplishing a goal
- The self-esteem of being somebody they are proud of

THE 4 HORSEMEN OF THE APOCALYPSE OF ALW
1. Fear
2. Greed
3. Envy
4. Impatience

WINNING...
- is an attitude
- is a commitment
- is a vision for your future – is a goal being met at a price
- is a symbol of your expectations
- is a way of life
- is an unconditional belief in yourself
- is a symbol of your expectations
- is a way of life
- is a way of tracking how you were doing
- is a positive reinforcement
- is faith in your future
- is a mental discipline
- is faith
- is a personal transformation
- is dynamic
- it create ideas
- it creates will power
- it's what life is all about
- it can't be ignored
- it determines how much you earn
- it determines how much you produce
- it determines the leaders you produce
- it takes patience and will be accomplished

- it's your resolve to win and see yourself winning
- is your belief in yourself
- is shown in your conviction
- it means you want to Be Somebody
- it means you want to be number one
- it means you are tired of losing.
- It means you are no longer average and ordinary
- it means you're doing it
- it means you are willing to do the nasty things over and over

THE MIND...
When a Person Joins:
- A person gets their body into the business. Then the person gets their mind into the business. Then a person gets their heart into the business.

When a Person Leaves:
- Their heart is the first to go. Then their mind goes. Then it's finally the body that leaves.

CORPORATIONS DON'T CAPTURE THE HEART
A corporation always has a man's body and mind but never his heart. This opportunity and crusade always allow him to put his heart into something.

3 FUNDAMENTALS
1. Stir It Up:
- The law of averages
- The law of large numbers of people
- Sheer hard work
- Make a decision

2. Do Something with It:
- Depth in recruiting is a priority
- The sharp edge of a new recruit's market, call with enthusiasm
- Spouse participation and commitment

3. Development of a Team:
- Have a positive attitude
- Use recognition
- Believing in your people
- Sell the dream
- Unconditional love and belief in yourself and your people

HAVE A GOAL OF GREATNESS IN YOUR LIFE.

12/9/1984
BOCA RATON, FL

OUR PURPOSE HERE
The original purpose of why ALW was founded…
- Is to improve lives: make extra money, have new homes and great lives
- There ain't no good jobs: people are tired of corporate America
- Build a company within a company
- Whatever Art does we should duplicate
- Why should you work? Because people are tugging at my heart strings.
- I'm in awe of what this opportunity can mean to so many

TO BE SPECIAL
- Make a contribution to something that will live beyond our lifetimes, a legacy that shows I existed, that I was here, that I made a difference
- I Love it, I don't just like it, I love it
- We really work for our people, our people don't work for us
- Our job is to make people feel special
- You must have total confidence that you will have victory
- I made an unconditional commitment
- This organization is making history
- Dream about conquering the world

A LEADER'S VOCABULARY
- Victory: Over what?
- Win: Who do you want to be?
- Succeed: What is your definition of success?
- Unconditional Commitment: To what?
- Conquer: Who's the foe?
- Leaders deliver for their people. The only thing you can give them is a dream.
- Leaders have whys
- Followers have hows

THE CRUSADE
- This business is not taught, it's caught
- Crusaders die hard
- This is our chance to make a difference
- How do you feel about what you do?
- Keep excitement in the business
- You must believe in something bigger than just your business
- Our crusade is our uniqueness

- We're dealing with people's lives and if you're not serious you better get serious about it.

HOW TO BUILD A BUSINESS
- Do what you do best: recruit to sell or sell to recruit
- Make money. Get yourself right financially
- Get confidence that you can make money
- Then become a builder
- Help others make money: "you will always make more money off of me than I will make off of you"
- Stop worrying: Leaders make friends with failure and embrace failure as a necessary means of learning.

Wherever you are, be great there. If you are a District, be a great District. Don't think so much about RVP that you don't perform at your current level.

UNWRITTEN LAWS OF WINNING
- See that all the bad plays have been taken out of our business
- Administration, security and credibility in leadership are all in place
- Timing is everything. The time is now to Be Somebody.
- Get your priorities in order: "I'm doing it for my family". You must be willing to give up ALW for your family.
- Give your energies time to compound
- Dream again. Your supply is equal to your demand if your demand is equal to the supplies availability
- What you sow is what you'll reap
- *You will get 10 times the yield on all your efforts. 50 direct recruits will yield 500 recruits. 10 direct recruits will yield 100. Go get 50!*
- Have a grateful heart
- Don't curse the darkness, light a candle
- Count your blessings
- Have an unconditional commitment
- Think big and choose to conquer the world.

THE CORPORATE WORLD
What they have now is discouraging to the person who has a vision, a dream and a true desire to Be Somebody.

UNCONDITIONAL COMMITMENT
- In good times and in bad
- For better or for worse
- Love people for who they are, not for what they do. That's the basis of unconditional commitment and love.

ART IS CONTROVERSIAL
He incites hatred in people because of the crusade, the cause, and the enemy, and that transforms people from indifference to ACTION.

LOVE THIS COMPANY
- Decide to stay in this company and work long enough until one person's life is transformed
- Pay one death claim
- Have one part-timer earn extra money and pay off all their debt
- Have one part-timer earn extra money to have their spouse quit work
- Have one person, because of you, earn 2 to 3 times what they were earning prior to this company

TO BUILD A NATIONWIDE COMPANY
- Recruit people for part-time income, but see them as RVPs and SVPs
- Sell the part-time income
- Sell a business of their own
- If you choose to be an RVP, then be the best damn RVP you can
- I choose to be the very best I can be and that's all I can do

ADVERSITY
Understand that something constructive is born out of adversity… it's a moment of time when ordinary men do something extraordinary.

AS ALW GOES, SO GOES THE COUNTRY
- Inflation and a struggling social security system are symptoms
- No pension programs in America cause worry
- If you do not bring the truth about money, finances, insurance, taxes to middle class America, who will?

FIRE IN THE BELLY
- It's gotten by association. It's who you associate with
- Big dreams only come from other people's dreams
- A log will only glow with the roaring logs that are burning to catch it on fire
- A bigger vision only comes from associating with bigger visionaries

- Find a hero
- We always play to the level of our competition
- Birds of a feather flock together
- Get a mastermind group – success is caught, not taught
- People are looking for leaders
- An association with dreamers causes you to dream, an association with losers causes you to lose
- A man is known by the company he keeps

SOMEBODY
The desire to Be Somebody can only be gotten by associating oneself with a person who has a burning desire that is so great, that it becomes contagious.
Two logs that are burning can add a third that will burn. Just as two logs burn, just take a third log an add it to the fire. To put it out, take the third log away from the other two.

ASSOCIATION
To decide and catch the fever of a fire in the belly, we must hear the dreams of another person. Like a shopping list. We decide what we want, by hearing what others want, we then add it to our list of goals. The fire in the belly can only be fueled by others.
A Mastermind group is comprises a larger mind, a larger ambition, a large addition which expands ours to the point of surpassing possibility.

7/23/1985
DALLAS, TX

- I want to Be Somebody so bad, I can taste it
- To really reach people's hearts you have to see them eyeball to eyeball
- This organization will never let you down
- It's tough to make $100,000 and be financially independent.
- If you can still dream, and still want to Be Somebody - you can
- Wake up every morning dreaming about building something gigantic
- I'm so proud to be part of this national championship team

WINNING IN A BUSINESS OF YOUR OWN
You are here for only a Flicker. Your gas tank of life is half full.
You do not have an unlimited opportunity to become somebody.
Be honest with yourself. Look at the last 10–20 years of your life. The next 10–20 will be the same. You can change your life in 90 days if you can still dream and hope.

OVERCOMING
It almost intimidated me. Getting into sales is intimidating.
- Desire: I wanted to be a champion more than anything else in the world.
- Have a positive attitude: It is the difference between average and ordinary and success

AN ABSOLUTE IN LIFE
- Attitude is the single most important thing you can develop on this earth
- 90% of winning is being excited
- Everything in life tells you not to be excited every day
- Be excited about your job – Be a dreamer again
- Life will turn out the way you see it turning out for you
- When was the last time you were excited about life?
- Charge ahead
- Smart people can't make it in business
- Just do it and do it and do it and do it until the job gets done, then talk about how great it is to Be Somebody that you are proud of and how you're not like everybody else.

CHARACTER
The depth of your character will be determined by the depth, degree, strength and desire of your vision. Character is only developed by overcoming obstacles, by overcoming doubt and overcoming rejection.

TO THOSE STRUGGLING
- This has become just a business to you
- The crusade has diminished
- The vision is weakened due to lack of discipline and renewal of your goals, aspirations, desires and dreams
- You end your struggle by setting a new goal

THE PRICE OF BEING A CRUSADER
- Rejection, Loneliness
- Misunderstanding, Doubt
- Decision, Commitment
- Vision

THE REWARDS OF BEING A CRUSADER
- Feeling of being special
- Financial freedom
- Security
- Positive self-esteem

7/24/1985

THE 80-20 RULE
- 80% of the people will do 20% of the work
- 20% of the people will do 80% of the work
- Our job is to build a company. We will have 80% ers, to get more 20% ers we need to find more 80%ers.

THE INFALLIBILITY OF SUCCESS HERE
Confidence for a Commitment: This will never fail you...
1. *Crusade:*
   - Whole life versus term
   - There ain't no good jobs
2. *The Opportunity to Progress:*
   - We guarantee your promotions if you do the work. This will never fail you.
3. *Our Market:*
   - Law of averages and geometric progression
4. *And YOU will be successful if:*
   - You can be a dreamer again
   - You pray for God's help
   - You have a positive attitude
   - You expect miracles
   - You are a husband and wife team

8/16/1985
MUNICH, GERMANY

- Brandeis: "If we would only realize life is hard, life would be easier to live."
- The purpose of any organization is to get results
- Just showing up is 80% of winning in ALW

CORPORATIONS ENCOURAGE DISLOYALTY
- They pay new people more than the old
- They promote from the outside
- They promote lesser qualified people

GOALS AND VISIONS
- A temporary step until you obtain the desired goal, a burning desire, a vision and a crusade
- The first goal should be financial: $100,000 invested in 10 years
- The magic of believing you will reach your goals.
- Pound this into your head: Accumulate $100,000 ASAP.

BIG PLAY
- In every game someone has to make the big play
- It can turn the momentum around. You have to make the big play.
- The big play is recruiting 10 team people in one month and recruiting deep
- The big play is personally doing $10,000 a month in personal premium
- YOU have to make the big play
- A big play can turn the momentum around
- Go out and become the "bell cow" of your organization

THAT'S THE WAY IT IS
- Why does a person get licensed and quit? That's the way it is.
- Why doesn't a person work hard? That's the way it is.
- Why don't people who need extra money come to work here? That's the way it is.
- Why doesn't an RVP get big? That's the way it is.
- Understanding the way it is doesn't change the reasons
- Health's spas? If everyone who belonged went, they would have no more room
- Churches? If everyone who belonged went, you wouldn't have enough room.

JERRY FALWELL SAID
"Greatness is not determined by talent, finances, assets, success. Greatness is determined by what it takes to discourage you, to get you to quit." Art: What little thing will it take to get you to quit? A chargeback, not making a sale, a person quitting, a broken appointment?

9/1/1985

COURAGE IS...
- Strength, the presence of mind against the odds, the determination to hang in there, to venture, to persevere, to withstand hardship, it's keeping power
- Courage is an inner test
- One more call after a discourteous appointment
- Working hard when you're broke and the pay statement shows a big chargeback that was unexpected
- Staying positive when no one shows up to the opportunity meeting
- A quiet resolve when your best recruit doesn't come to a fast start school
- The determination that must come when your best recruit quits
- That silent struggle to go on against seemingly hopeless odds

- The desire to persist when you see a look on your spouse's face that suggests you should quit
- To work long hard hours and not have any success, but you continue to work
- Courage is the presence of fear and you do it anyway
- When you are fearful of failing and fearful of succeeding, but you maintain a positive attitude
- Taking out a mutual fund when you can't seem to afford it
- Giving back the policies to a client that will not give you a good commitment
- Seeing the positives in things when only the negatives are evident
- To maintain your vision when all around you are negative

BE POSITIVE
Concentrate on the good things, dwell on what's good:
- see the good in people
- see the positives in the business
- see the positives in the law of averages
- see the positives in geometric progression
- thankfulness is the opposite of bitterness

If your ratios decrease, you don't believe in what you're doing. The depth of your beliefs actualize in the width of your results.

ENTHUSIASM
Enthusiasm: nothing great happens without being excited

11/1/1985

BE A DREAMER AGAIN
- Seek financial freedom
- Don't sweat the small stuff
- Freedom from a boss or a job
- In business for yourself
- No time clock to punch
- Have unlimited income
- Secure your future and income
- Build equity in your life and feel important, make a difference in the lives of other people, have a chance to Be Somebody
- Have a definite promotion system to get ahead
- Live an exciting life. Be on a mission or have purpose in your life
- Work when you want to work
- Having pride in what you do and what you've accomplished

- Build a business that you have the responsibility for
- Help other people
- Be Somebody that you are proud of
- Have it all
- Have a chance in your life
- Have hope
- Make your life count
- Be responsible for the fact that thousands of people are financially independent because of you

11/16/1985

POSITIVE WINNING ATTITUDE
- You are born to win
- The first step is being thankful for what you have, seeing the good in your current life
- Attitude is the way you look at life
- Call 10 get one; two ways to look at it. Be negative about the nine or positive about the one
- You can't be positive without a vision of what you want, a goal, a dream, something you have a reason to be positive about

ALW WAS FORMED
- To give people like me and you a chance at financial independence and a new prosperous life
- To build security for us and our families
- To give hope that it will get better
- To live the kind of lives we want to live
- To do something special with their lives
- To give you a chance to Be Somebody

LAW OF AVERAGES THE GREAT EQUALIZER OF ALW
- Sometime in your ALW career, you won't be able to dream like you should, believe like you should, work like you should
- When all else fails, you fall to some lull, it is there where you make up your mind and believe
- The law of averages is that guarantee
- Someone will buy, someone will join
- People are going to do what they're going to do

HOW TO SET AND ACHIEVE A GOAL
- Be around goal setters
- Listen to their dreams, their futures, their organization
- It's contagious
- Get around money motivated people, you'll become them
- You don't lack goals, you lack ideas to get hooked on
- Life will give you what you are willing to fight for
- Give your efforts time to compound

COMMITMENT
Don't quit – all winners have more failures then losers do

SUCCESS
Success comes the day you decide that you and your family deserve better, deserve trips, deserve going to Europe, deserve going to Hawaii, deserve the home of your dreams.

CHOICE
Life is a choice. You change your thinking and you change your life.

Art Williams: Part 6

KANSAS CITY AND NEW ORLEANS

1990

ART WILLIAMS: PART 6

1/24/1990
NSD MEETING
KANSAS CITY, MO

THINK LIKE A WINNER
- People are betting millions of dollars on us.
- I want to be part of something great. I don't want to be around complainers and whiners.
- There has never been a company that gives the number of families success as much as we do.
- To our critics: "Who the hell are you, with your success record, to question what this company is and what we will become?"
- The odds are against people making it in business, or even making $100,000 a year.
- The average income of an NSD is $396,000
- This company has delivered
- We are the number one life insurance company in the world
- We are the number one mutual fund company in the world
- The success of our people is incredible

CAN YOU FIND ANOTHER COMPANY WITH THIS KIND OF OPPORTUNITY?
- Name another company that gives people a chance to make this kind of money?
- Do you defend this company?
- When people complain about us and the fact that some are not making money, do you defend this company?
- Shame on you for how this company delivered for you and you let people run this company down
- This company is built for the ball busters. The people who are tired of corporate America tattooing them.
- I love everything about this company. I love the crusade, The toughness, the reward, the system.
- The company is always trying to give the field the extra edge.
- Have pride in all that ALW is, does, offers, gives, provides, endures and compensates.
- This company is designed to help families make money and save money
- Most leaders in ALW want more for doing less. If you don't produce, you can't hide with our compensation system.
- We have the most honest compensation program in America.
- Without this company, this country is in a world of hurt

A CRUSADER, HIS MISSION AND HIS PASSION
These elements give you the extra commitment, the extra courage, the extra desire, the extra staying power. Some of us are making it big because we've got substance in our hearts.
When you are committed to anything, like we are, great things happen.

Mickey Mantle:
"If you like something you can never be good at it. You have got to love it."

- Our compensation system pays you to produce business, produce leaders and to FIGHT
- To be Wealthy you must bust your butt, build 7–10 RVPs and bust your butt some more. Fight until you win.
- Always CHARGE
- A company, products, compensation doesn't win for you, it's up to you. How much do you believe?

Identify winners, people that are loyal, and put them on a pedestal. Losers and Duds should be treated great. Never give up on them… but never listen to them.

- The state of the company is great
- It will get better but we don't need to have it better
- Your Wealth is determined by your efforts
- Stand on your own two feet and be held accountable to the amount of money you make.

America is designed to take care of mediocre people. Not ALW. We give everybody a chance to do it. We put a uniform on anyone that wants it. And they can go as far as they want to go. Passion, toughness, pride. I love it, I love to talk about it.

- This concept, this environment, this opportunity, this system gave me a chance to be financially independent.
- There is a danger in the gold mine of overrides, making something off of someone else. You could go and cool it.
- For weak people it's hard to keep busting it.
- If you ever think this company owes you something, you are a has been

- Until we win, I will do whatever it takes.

The day you are not willing to do what a District Leader has to do, you are a has been.

WE NEED
- a new vision
- a new pride
- a new commitment
- a new attitude
- a new mission
- new energy
- a new effort

- As long as you wear this uniform, I will never stop believing in you
- We can carry this crusade around the world, dominate the world
- I need hundreds of people to capture the spirit, to love this company with an intensity you can't believe. We can conquer the world.

- NSD is a prestigious position
- I'm so happy that we didn't quit like other people quit
- I'll fight for you. You are one of us.
- I'm so proud to have you as a teammate

Our SYSTEM will penalize you for being a pansy when it comes to your love for this company.

If you're not proud to be part of this team, you will fade away.

Losers aren't impressed with us because they've never been a winner. Winners are impressed because they know what it takes to win.

CHALLENGE
A challenge is a lack of confidence that we could do what we did again, again, again

- You NSDs are the princes of this company. As you go so does the company.
- A worry is that unless you have fun you can't last long. If you're not happy and don't love it, you'll never do something historic.
- Our greatest strength is the youth of our top leaders
- Live a balanced life
- Work with intensity when you work
- Delegate your problems

- Don't feel sorry for the losers and quitters
- Attitude and activity are the only things we can control
- Keep a fabulous attitude

- Don't listen to the losers
- Be more grateful and thankful
- Be happier
- Get strong fundamentally
- Recruit the right market

- Raise your expectations
- Have big base shops
- Have a goal of 30 sales minimum a month in your base shop, 10 recruits per month, $10,000 in premium per month and 10 direct legs producing each month
- Build Crusaders: Build pride back into your base

ART'S MANAGEMENT PRINCIPLES
1. Build fighters
2. Save money and cut costs
3. Put NSDs on a pedestal; these are our heroes
4. Your people do as you do
5. Be able to handle the success of being successful
6. Challenge people to be controversial, because that's what we are

The thing that amazes me about marginal people, they can't make it here, but they think it's easier somewhere else. If you can't make it here, you can't make it anywhere.

Fact: I've never met anyone who has left this company where the upline wasn't better off.

- General Patton: "If you want people to remember what you say, you've got to say it in a dramatic way".

- If you want on my Elite Team plant your feet, look somebody in the eye and CHARGE

TO BUILD A LEGENDARY HIERARCHY
- You've got to be a crusader
- Take charge of your destiny and do it yourself
- Spend 90% of your time in the field. Go 7–10 wide and 4 deep
- Build with greenies
- Build strong personal relationships
- Always be a positive happy person and show it all the time
- Master the art of praise, always have a good word for people
- Master recruiting
- Sell the part-time dream. This is the greatest part-time opportunity in the history of the world. Prepare people to come full-time
- Recruit the spouse
- Be smart and be a good business person. The business will be a nightmare if you don't
- My business made me wealthy and will make you wealthy too.
- Invest in your business not in speculative things
- You have to have local heroes, somebody to put on a pedestal
- Be a success in your personal life. You don't have to be perfect but you've got to make your family a priority
- Compete don't compare because the enemy of jealousy will eat you up
- Compete with your personal goals
- Prune the dead butts out of your organization, not firing, but pruning
- Always keep the new tigers coming
- Remember, it only takes a few
- Look at any little thing as a sign that this is going to be your record year. The energy then comes out of you.

- In my darkest hour, I said to myself "You are only one stud away from a surge"
- Give your efforts time to compound

There is always hope when you RECRUIT.

3/7/1990
NEW ORLEANS CONVENTION

- 35,000 people in attendance
- This is truly an historic meeting
- We are a close, tough-knit company. There is a oneness with this company
- Do things you are good at over and over and over and over

THE DREAM IS GIVING FAMILIES
- A chance to make money
- A chance to build a gigantic override income
- A chance to build a company within a company
- A chance to become financially independent
- But, you can't play if you are on the sideline

A COMPANY OF DESTINY
- Having 50 good people in your organization in 1990 will pay you $1 million a year
- The mystique in this company is the RVP position. It is a symbol of success in your community
- Put RVPs on a pedestal
- There is power in multiple replacements
- The replacement formula must be mastered

DO IT
- Build 7–10 key people in 12 months
- Do $10,000 a month minimum premium; 10 recruits a month; 10 direct legs producing
- Get good replacements
- When leaders quit, when your best guy quits, think about it for 22 seconds, then replace them with two better people.
- Winners don't "almost" anything. They don't lose – losing is unacceptable.
- Victory is our desire
- No one will deny me my opportunity to win
- Sell out: 8 to 10 hours a day

ATTACK
- Be proud. Be tough. Attack!

ATTACK!!!
- Pride and love ooze out of us. That's what made us successful.
- You recruit people to you, not mutual funds, not insurance, not the the company, but to you
- Your pride oozing out of you recruits the people
- Be sold out to the effort and the building

- I want a war, I'm a soldier, I'm looking for a battle
- When you attack, you turn negatives into weapons
- The personal touch means we are a company of listeners, we are a company with heart, we are a company with a personal touch, we care! You are this company to your people.
- Our company motto? "ALW, where the sales people are King"

- Most corporations are run by pretty people who look down their noses at us

THREE KEYS TO BUILDING PERSONAL RELATIONSHIPS
1. Recruit greenies
2. Spend your time with your people
3. Always sell the dream. Together we can conquer the world

LOVE THE TOUGHNESS
- The only thing we will leave behind in life is the influence we have made on others
- God: "Keep me first and all the rest will come."
- You only win as long as you perform
- You are number one, can you stand to be number two?
- You make money by doing the tough things
- The person that wins is just going to want it a little bit more
- I wanted it bad
- All my life I wanted people to look at me and think I'm special, to say to me "you are a winner"
- Be proud, be tough, attack. Thank goodness it's tough.

ALW IS BUILT
1. For the ball busters
2. For the 2%ers
3. For people that want to Be Somebody

THE COMMON DENOMINATORS OF WINNERS
- they are super hard workers
- they are super intense
- they are super dedicated
- they are super tough

- Good enough does not mean you are tough enough
- Tough means never showing hurt or doubt while you are hurting or doubting
- Tough is being excited and happy when you don't feel like it
- The world says get a job, be ordinary, be comfortable. Comfort makes the world feel better about themselves because they are ordinary.

TOUGH AND PROUD
Are you tough? Are you proud to attack, or are you a pansy?
- Tough means never giving up
- Tough means being aggressive
- Tough means never retreating
- Tough means recruiting 4 down where you can work harder

- Tough means always charging, charging and improving. That gives you the extra edge

ATTACK - TURN NEGATIVES INTO WEAPONS
- You wake up every day with a knot in your stomach
- Attack is a mental attitude – if you want to be the best you can be, you can't be beat.
- The enemy isn't the insurance industry, its not Prudential, it is…….
- it's getting too comfortable – it's retreating
- it's resting on your laurels
- it's your attitude, and expectancy
- it's complaining
- it's accepting good when you could be great

ART'S THOUGHTS
- Have a recruiting mindset
- It's a team not an organization
- Have a high expectancy: districts doing 10,000 divisions 20,000 RVP's doing 30,000
- Have a high level of expectancy
- Husband and wife commitment
- Every quarter get momentum going
- Be committed to your goals and read them every day
- Blitz: sell them on why they want to recruit
- Total intensity. Do it and get it over with
- Be totally coachable. Be a maniac on a mission

Art Williams: Part 7

WINNING AND COMMITMENT

1985-1990

ART WILLIAMS: PART 7
- **WINNING TALK**
- **COMMITMENT**
- **JUST DO IT**
- **DIFFERENCE BETWEEN $50k AND $500k RVP**

10/22/1985
NSD MEETING
NEW HOME OFFICE - DULUTH, GA

GREATNESS
- This company is prepared for greatness
- We've got a war going on. The war room is the most privileged meeting room in this company.
- Everybody in the world has the same problems
- Winners handle fears, frustration, self-doubt, they get scared like everybody else
- You are never going to solve all your problems
- The bigger you get, the bigger the problems get
- Doing something special with your life causes big problems
- Winning is the ability to handle your problems and be happy
- The goal in life is to be happy

- I'm not as excited as I ought to be, or as positive as I ought to be
- I ought to be excited and I'm worried about some little piddly thing
- We have a chance to do something gigantic in America

- We have to do a better job of not letting the problems get in our way. Not let these problems get us down.
- Don't let the losers change us. We are going to be excited and enthusiastic
- NSD – the highest paid executives in America.

ART'S POINTS
Get in the building business and continue to grow. Talk to 10 times as many people in a positive way. Concentrate on the good things in A.L.Williams.

WHAT TO BE EXCITED ABOUT
- Be grateful. Dwell on what is good, not on what is bad.
- We are an institution
- ALW corporation has a line of credit of $67.5 million
- There are 44 institutions now investing in ALW
- The finest product in the industry

- Mass recruiting – Other companies do not like it.
- Hiring greenies – People that want to Be Somebody – We brought this to the industry.
- Our average age is 33, the industry average 38
- We can handle $150 billion in life insurance administratively
- The TV network is a go – March 1986
- 18 to 20 lawsuits? That's nothing. It's insignificant. All companies have lawsuits.
- Nothing can destroy ALW. There may be one bad person in ALW but there are thousands of good people.

REASONS TO BE EXCITED
- Products. Administration. Money. Production. TV network.
- International expansion - 48 people from Canada toured the home office.
- ALW corporation and office support
- Our future we will be in New York. Cheaper products. Mutual funds in July 1986

16 YEARS AGO TODAY ART STARTED
- Better market – there is more business to replace today than 16 years ago
- 300,000 agents are prospecting for us. They sell more every day than we can sell in our lifetime.
- People deserve and we give them our best
- I'm not quitting. I'm here for the duration
- All the crap and vicious things we had to go through are now over
- Anyone who quits today is a fool. A quitting mentality is when you quit competing or caring.
- We have a chance to make our greatest contributions
- I want to conquer the world
- Hundreds of thousands of people are counting on us. As ALW goes so does America.
- We are the consumers only hope
- It's lonely at the top
- Grow up

WINNING
You win with greenies who are afraid, scared, who doubt themselves, and are not superstars.

11/12/1985

TO WIN IN THE FREE ENTERPRISE SYSTEM
- Become a better person
- Go to work on you. You can change your life. There is still time left to change.
- You must have desire. God instills it in you at birth
- Aren't you supposed to Be Somebody? If you hunger to Be Somebody, and never quit dreaming, you will Be Somebody.
- Develop one thing, a positive winning attitude
- It comes from being tough, vicious, and doing the nauseating work you have to do
- It is the key to victory in business and in your personal life
- You must have an excited attitude about life
- People won't follow a dull, disillusioned, negative, dadgum crybaby
- To WIN you need to be positive, excited and pumped up
- 90% of winning is being excited. Especially when you don't feel like being excited.
- Hard? Everything in life tells you to be negative.
- Two ways to look at life, bad or good
- As long as there is a breath left in me I choose to be positive
- You must develop the ability to dream. Pay the price: you've got to start working.

5/1/1987 - DALLAS, TX

KEY TO STAYING MOTIVATED
- I'm so pumped up, I'm so proud of this company
- Art, why do you keep going, where do you get your motivation?
- You the people. You are my motivation, my love, my joy.
- Corporate America put people like me down and told I wasn't supposed to make a lot of money

INTENSITY
- If you want to Be Somebody with an intensity that borders on being fanatical, you will
- Key to winning? Inside qualities
- ALW isn't a business, this is a family, this is my life. I want to die on the job.
- We have a window of opportunity to do something good for America
- I pray to God to give us what we need to help this country
- I don't promise you it will be easy, I promise you it will be worth it

- If you don't accept losing, you will succeed
- I wish you could feel my intensity
- We are not talking about buy term and invest the rest. It's about you doing something special and big. You are going to want to quit 100 times and go out and get a good job.
- I don't blow smoke
- ALW is a family
- If you believe you are going to win you will
- I came to Dallas to talk about your lives
- What's your life worth?
- You aren't going to luck yourself into winning
- You are not going to talk yourself into winning

Your life is just a Flicker. Time is running out.

- You can bet your life on this company
- I'm an expert on winning
- If you want to win, if you can still believe, if you've been hurt and put down too many times? If there is still a fire in you, if you can still dream, still get excited, if you can believe one more time?
- Look at the last 10 to 15 years of your life and if you don't change, nothing will change.
- This is the way I want to live my life
- ALW is not built to beat Prudential or make history. It was built for you and your family to make some real money, save some real money, and build a business.
- Are you a winner? Are you a 2%er?
- ALW was not built for everyone to win

TALKING WINNING IS TALKING A DIFFERENT LANGUAGE
- It's easy to say it, but it's hard to do it
- Words like loyal, committed, paying the price, you think you understand it
- Everyone wants a nice home, to go to Europe and be financially independent
- Life gives you what you accept and what you fight for
- You've got to want to be a somebody with an intensity that is almost fanatical
- Somebody's say "you're supposed to make a difference with your life, to go for it, to commit to something."
- You are going to be the change that you need
- A leader can't win for you, your up line can't win for you, you win for you
- It starts with your attitude to be a winner

- You don't have to be a superstar to win.

Smart people have a hard time winning because they're always trying to figure things out.

DESIRE
- The key is desire
- How bad do you want to Be Somebody?
- How tough will you fight?
- How often will you pick yourself up after you've been knocked down?

HEART
- The key is your heart
- Are you a good person?
- Can people count on you? Do unto others as you would have others do unto you.

ATTITUDE
- The key is your attitude
- Can you stay positive?
- Can you stay excited? Everybody would love to win. But they aren't good enough.

THINK AND GROW RICH
- You must have a specific dream
- As Think and Grow Rich teaches…
  - Make it specific
  - Have a specific time
  - Write it down
  - Develop a plan to attain it
  - Decide what price you're willing to pay to get it
  - Think about reaching your goal every day

WANT TO WIN? DO THIS
- I am OBSESSED with becoming financially independent
- I can't be what I want to be the way I'm going
- Your ability to pick yourself up time after time after time
- Reward and Punish yourself

Don't quit:
All you can do is all you can do and all you can do is enough….

All I heard my first year was no, no, no, no, no,. I felt like such a dud...a loser.

ALL YOU CAN DO
- All you can do is all you can do and all you can do is enough.
- Are you doing all you can do? Then it's enough.

DO WHATS RIGHT
- You are doing what is right.
- Everyone is not going to buy or join
- Enough people will buy and will join and you will become financially independent

ACTION PRINCIPLES
- Always do it first
- Always do what you want your people to do
- Make money
- Recruit
- Stay positive

STAGES TO WINNING
It takes 3 to 5 years in business to get a toe-hold.
The first 18 months encompass these stages:
- Lying stage
- Quitting stage
- Endurance stage

The above are the three stages of winning where you find out that you have to burn all your bridges.

I went to bed scared every day. I was sick every day.

OTHERS AND COMPETITION
- You can't worry about what others think, say or do
- What your family says
- What the inside competition is like
- What the outside competition is doing

THE WINNING EDGE
- You beat 50% of the people by working hard
- 40% by doing what's right and being a good person
- 10% is a dogfight

BE A GREAT LEADER
- Don't worry about things you can't control like war, inflation, the government.
- Be a risk taker where you learn by doing, have the guts to make mistakes
- Be a good person - do what's right, honor commitments, tell the truth
- Treat people good:
  - Always look for the good in everybody
  - Praise and recognition are great motivators
- Be loyal and stand for something: don't be a pansy
- People won't believe in a fence sitter or a mealy mouth
- Get emotionally involved
- You WIN with your heart, not your head
- Body language is more powerful than verbal language…
- Always keep doing the things that make you successful…
  - Recruiting
  - Field training
  - Selling the dream
- You can't let fear stop you or keep you from trying
- Most people don't try because they are afraid to fail

EVERYBODY BATTLES
- Everybody gets scared and worries every day
- Everybody in the world everyday has:
  - self doubt, insecurity, worry, fear

Every successful person in the world is confident for only hours at a time…

REALIZE
- This is a Numbers business: People that do the most, make the most
- People that recruit the most make the most.
- Keep them coming and keep them going.
- Attitude is everything:
  - Always be excited
  - Always be positive
  - Always be enthusiastic…
  - Don't let the bitchers, the criers, and the complainers ruin you.
  - Live for the good people. Give your best to those who are "doing it."

YOU ARE NOT
- a marriage counselor
- an administrator
- a psychologist
- a banker
- a mediator
- a babysitter

YOU ARE
- a Leader
- a Motivator
- a Builder
- an Honest, Sincere example of a balanced life.
- a Winner

BE TOUGH
I will give you my toughness, my ability, my time, but I will not give you my money.

Tough times don't last, tough people do.

ALW IS LIKE A FOOTBALL TEAM...ATTITUDE OF A WINNING FOOTBALL TEAM
- Football doesn't mean as much to the other teams as it does to us
- The other teams aren't as tough as our team
- Either you will win or the other guy will win
- Who will win? The one who loves it the most, it's an attitude.
- They don't love it like you love it
- They're not as tough as we are
- If you want to quit and die, then do it. This team will leave you behind.
- If you want to feel sorry for yourself, we're going to leave you behind
- Our team hits them with more intensity than ever before
- Our team is moving, we work on holidays, and on weekends
- Every time there was a bad article we shoved it down their throat

Winners never get bored with the basics.

ART'S PHILOSOPHY
- Have a childlike enthusiasm
- Always see the positive in things
- Be disciplined
- Be flexible

- Perform consistently
- Make decisions and SELL your people on it
- Set realistic goals and achieve them
- Praise one on one; criticize in a group
- Never make excuses for failures
- Give your team credit for success and take the blame for failure
- Avoid being in the spotlight
- Avoid bragging
- Be Art to all the people you touch
- There are no bad people just bad RVPs
- We are all looking for a role model
- Become the person you want to copy

5/2/1987

WINNERS VS LOSERS
- Winners bet their lives on something for real
- Winners realize it takes time and it's going to be tough
- Winners make promises and commitments to their people and work hard to keep them
- Winners look into the mirror and realize that for things to change they have to change
- Winners look at themselves to solve their problems
- Winners work when they don't feel like working
- Winners realize they need a leader
- Winners are dependent upon leaders
- Winners are not loners, they go to all the meetings
- Winners feel strong about what they do
- Winners are committed to do the hard work
- Winners love to compete
- Winners make something happen
- Winners push and challenge their people to be the best they can be
- Winners want you to win
- Winners step it up, they don't want to just play the role
- Winners have a lot of heartache
- Winners are not the pretty people

ART'S FEARS AND HIS TOTAL COMMITMENT
- I live in fear that I'm not a good enough a leader to motivate you and encourage you
- I don't want to be just another company, I want it to be the best company it can be for you
- 10 years ago I looked at Art Williams and I didn't like what I saw
- I want to Be Somebody with an intensity that is almost fanatical

- I took my adventures for granted
- If I had to do it over again I would have worked harder, loved it more, gave more of myself
- I looked at my coaching record and I was sad. I didn't do what I could have done
- I should have worked harder, believed more, tried harder
- I looked in the mirror. I was pretty good. I didn't want to be pretty good, I wanted to look into that mirror and say "that's a stud."
- Fear of failure keeps most people from trying
- I didn't win like I wanted to win, I'm not sure what I would have done
- I always held something in reserve. I didn't know if I was good enough.
- I'm sick and tired of second guessing myself
- I'm going to try and lay it on the line and try one more time
- I made a decision that one time in my life, before I die, that I can do it
- Art Williams likes Art Williams
- There is still time for you to win if you commit

4 THINGS THAT CAUSE UNHAPPINESS
1. Panic management decisions
2. Bad personal financial situations
3. Lack of activity; you can't depend on any one thing… one sale… or one recruit
4. Lack of a specific goal

You've got to be happy! To win, you've got to get emotional.

- How do you feel about what you're doing?
- Feeling good about what you do is electric

GET EXCITED
Get excited! "No one will follow a dull, disillusioned, dadgum crybaby." To lead, be inspired. The biggest turn off to people is unhappiness.

HAPPY BASE SHOP
- All things bad in sales come from being full-time too quick.
- Our part-time position is the greatest part-time income in America
- You need a happy base shop, *an unhappy base shop comes from too many full timers who lack activity*
- Sales people are unemployed every day
- Managers have security

Prospecting is a problem but recruiting through your people solves your prospecting problem. Therefore you are happy.

- People are fed up with high pressure, hard closing, insurance men
- Hard sales is going for the throat
- I want to deliver for my people. That makes me happy.
- I love it, not just like it
- ALW has no protected territory

TO BE HAPPY
- Be a good personal money earner
- Have someone to see every day
- Have direction and have a BIG goal
- Be a Crusader. Crusaders are happy people.
- Do it first. People respond to what you do, not what you say
- Save money, make money. This is an endurance contest. You're not going to win big without paying a big price.
- Having a team creates happiness
- You can't be happy if you're tattooing people

5/3/1987

Motivation is everything…

WINNERS AND LOSERS
What is the common denominator of a winner?
What is the difference between winners and losers?
- The difference is so thin and the separation is so thin
- You can do 99% of the things right and still not win
- The winning edge is mental toughness. MENTAL toughness comes from doing the tough things over and over
- Winners do it and do it and do it and do it and do it
- Losers think the winners are just at the right place at the right time and things just happened to work out for the winners
- Losers think they are the only ones who are scared, who lose sales, whose people quit them
- Winners hurt, fear, doubt and are scared, and people tell them no too
- But they do two things that the losers refuse to do: They don't quit but they want to.
- They have a will to win
- They have a desire to Be Somebody so much it's almost fanatical
- Just wanting to be successful isn't good enough

- Life will give you what you accept, good or bad

GARY PLAYER
At a tournament someone said to him – "I would give anything to hit a golf ball just like you".
Gary - "No you wouldn't – you would if it were easy. Nothing good comes without a lot of pain"
Gary - "Would you?"
- "get up at 5 AM like me?"
- "hit balls until your hands bleed, like I do?"
- "hit a 1,000 balls a day like me?"

WINNERS
- Winners can't stand being average and ordinary
- They can't stand the thought of living a wasted life

- Attitude is all there is… You don't like your status in life?
- Change your attitude. You can do it.
- Attitude only comes with hard work and a decision. A tough, cruel, sacrificial decision to do it.

HOW TO DEVELOP A POSITIVE ATTITUDE
- Get excited: 90% of winning is being excited to the point of looking like a fool
- A winner stays excited for as long as it takes to succeed and win
- Always be positive
- Become a dreamer again and be a goal setter
- The last period of life when people are dreamers is high school and college
- Most people keep taking what LIFE dishes out
- See yourself winning. Don't just see unhappiness, failure and disappointment.
- See good things happening to you

TOTAL COMMITMENT
- What is the difference between a $50,000 RVP and a $500,000 RVP? The $500,000 RVP just does it and does it and does it and does it until the job gets done
- They have the same contract, training, age, talent, family, speaking ability
- They both do everything they're supposed to do; they are loyal, they are good people, they are good sales people
- **They both do it, but the $500,000 earner does it and a little bit more.**
    - *Works hard and a little bit more*

- *Pays the price and a little bit more*
- *Is loyal and a little bit more*
- *Is tough and a little bit more makes*
- *Makes money and a little bit more. Saves money and a little bit more*

DESIRE
Establish the right kind of priorities to get out of life what you want. You've got to desire to win in your total life or you're not going to be the person you want to be.

DO IT... BE A LEADER
Anything that is successful has a leader. Leadership is enough.

Leaders do it. They do whatever it takes to get the job done. They do it, they do it, they do it, they do it, they do it. Then they talk about how great it is to Be Somebody they are proud of and how they are not like everybody else.

JUST DO IT!
- You can count on me to be an RVP. Great, just do it.
- I'm going to be number one. Great, just do it
- I'm going to be a district
- If I had just one good month
- If I could just sell my house
- If I could just get one good person
- If I could just make some money
- I'm going to win the trip to Europe
- I'm going to get appointments
- Where do you get appointments? Just get them
- I'm going to get 20 recruits this month
- When can I stop doing it? When I become an RVP? When I make enough money? No!
- I'm an RVP can I quit now? I'm an SVP can I quit? No, you can't quit.
- I don't have enough training
- My RVP doesn't help me

The primary difference between winners and losers? The winners they do it and they do it and they do it until the job gets done and then they talk about how great it is to Be Somebody that they are proud of and how they are not like everybody else.

5/5/1987

BE A PRODUCER AND NOT A TALKER
- I don't want to be part of a humdrum existence. I want to make a difference with my life.
- ALW is an opportunity for those who want to bust their butts
- We are going to produce a group of people that are producers and not talkers
- My job is not to get you to like me, my job is to get you to win
- You can't live your lives trying to please people
- You've got to be the right kind of person to make the opportunity work for you
- You give a stud freedom, and he seems to make things happen
- Go and do something fantastic
- We all need to produce and compete for our own mental well-being
- We are dream sellers
- We ultimately have to show people success by succeeding

5/18/1987

WHAT WINNERS DO TO BE STUDS
They dream big:
- Dream BIG because life turns out for you the way you see it turning out
- A winner goes through the same frustration, and disappointment as the losers
- They stay excited because people will not follow a dead butt
- It's easy to get negative
- You can work hard and still fail
- You can give a great presentation and still fail
- You can be the best trainer and still fail
- When you hurt or are mad, you stay excited
- You do this, especially when times are tough

THE ABILITY TO KEEP IT SIMPLE
- Winners realize there are no tricks
- Just hard work and keep from being frustrated. 8-5-3-1
- You can make more money working outside your comfort zone than at any company in America
- Follow the Golden rule and be a good person

DREAM BIG
- Always sell ALW as a life-changing event
- When you see yourself, see yourself winning and accomplishing the things that make you different. It unlocks your mental capacities
- Understand the awesomeness of this opportunity

6/8/1987

TO WIN
- You only have to have a small percentage of things work out to win big, really big
- To win: You need to stand for something and make a commitment
- A commitment is the ability to pick yourself up off the mat one more time

8/7/1987
DALLAS SUPER SEMINAR

GAME PLAN TO WIN
- The first 18 months everything you do turns to stink
- Years 2-5 you establish yourself
- Then things start to compound and multiply
- Compounding:
  - Years 1-10 accumulate $200,000
  - The next 2 to 3 years accumulate another $200,000
  - The next 1 year accumulate another $200,000

ALW BUILT FOR 2%ers
- ALW is not built for everyone to win
- It's built for winners to win
- Everyone won't pay the price to make it
- You can't take a donkey and win the Kentucky Derby
- You can't teach a pig to sing
- It looks simple and easy but it's a competitive desire and requires you fight and come back countless times from adversity

THE THING THAT GIANTS DO
- They run their business well and build a company within a company
- For a stud, freedom is essential. For a dud it hurts. They don't want to make decisions.
- Being big isn't bad

- Freedom can cause frustration
- Making exceptions for promotions comes from a slowdown in recruiting and panic management

RESPONSIBILITIES OF AN RVP
- Don't screw your people
- Do it legally
- Write good quality business

TIME MANAGEMENT
- 25% in office
- 75% wandering around making something happen

PROMOTION GUIDELINES & FREEDOM
- Promotion guidelines are the minimum you have to do
- Premature promotions by exceptions should be rare
- People must warrant a promotion and not be given a promotion
- It's the RVP's decision but they must earn the promotion
- RVP's must deliver on any promises of a promotion

WHEN TO MAKE A PREMATURE PROMOTION
- When people go full-time
- When they are great at sales and are average recruiters
- Use a combination of sales and recruits to get them promoted
- Give them 30 day goals
- For Special leaders who are unbelievable studs
- Just to blitz, to make something happen. An example is "five sales this month, etc. and you get a promotion to the next level."

3/9/1988
NSD MEETING

GROW UP
- At this stage in my career I'm not willing to work with negative people
- I will only work with positive, excited people who have goals
- I come to work thinking about conquering the world and you're worried about an administration problem?
- I'm talking about doubling your income. Tripling your income.
- Conquering the world. Going international.
- I can't do all that and deal with district leader attitudes
- I'm through being negative and pampering negative people
- No one can motivate you but you
- I want to identify a group of people around me that want to get big

- Feel good about your company, your future, and the magnitude of what we're about to do
- I have feelings every day that I just want to quit and go get a good job
- We all want to be small, but not too small
- Is it worth it? But I think "what am I going to do with my life?"
- Where can I go to do the exciting things I do?
- Where can I go to have that many people believe in me, listen to me, trust that much in me?

BE A STUD
- There is a major need in America for us to belong to something
- People don't feel good about themselves, who they are associated with or what they stand for
- Put all your problems out of your mind for the next 24 hours
- Making money is the scoreboard, but it's not happiness
- You have a group of people around you that will love you, care about you, support you
- You are wanting to be part of the special group of people aren't you?
- You want to be part of this group especially during the tough times, right?

TO BE HAPPY
- Work very hard
- Make tons of money
- Save tons of money; You can't be happy if you blow all your money
- Get some pressures off of you by making money
- Get a secretary
- Get a maid
- Take a family vacation
- Reward yourself every three years in a special way

BIG BASE SHOP
- The base shop is the magnet that attracts people and grows your business
- If you don't focus on a strong base shop you get worn out and will not be fulfilled
- Build a big, fun base shop
- Recognize your people
- Challenge your people
- Have big conventions and a big retreat and you'll touch peoples lives in a special way

TO WIN
Never take things personally. Everything can't be lovey dovey in your relationships.

YOUR RESPONSIBILITY
- To work and make a contribution that you will feel good about
- You are supposed to be positive, happy and loyal
- Teach your people the fundamentals of winning.
- We are not a sales company. Teach your people how to recruit.
- Be an example of how to treat people good and train them on it
- We are ready to do something big
- Because of the kind of people we are - be an example of treating people good
- Keep praising people
- Don't ever quit and always do something
- You lose when you stop working and recruiting

ALW GOALS
- The number one goal is to build financial independence for your family
- Have a specific goal
- Have a specific plan
- People need my attitude, they need my leadership, my excitement, my praise, my beliefs and my crusade
- Build total wealth for your family by building financially independent RVPs
- Push up people. We judge greatness by how many successful RVPs you produce
- We get down and depressed because we really don't think it's going to work and that comes from a slowdown in recruiting
- The real joy in this business is developing some studs and taking pride in watching them grow and succeed
- During your roller coaster ride have a goal that keeps you from getting depressed
- Success is a goal worth fighting for
- Believe in your heart that in 10 years you'll be earning $1M–2M dollars a year. Now that's worth fighting for
- Sell the dream and build a team

- Give your efforts time to compound
- Never forget where you came from
- You are constantly being challenged. This makes you rise to the occasion if you are a winner.
- Criticism makes you better

We don't have a job, we have a DESTINY.

3/11/1988
TARRANT COUNTY CONVENTION CENTER
FT. WORTH, TX

THE BIG LEAGUES IS YOUR LIFE
- The key to winning in life is attitude
- The big leagues is your life. It's not the NBA, NFL, major league baseball. It's your life.
- Your life is just a Flicker. There is not an unlimited number of opportunities out there.
- ALW is the greatest opportunity you'll ever see

WINNING IS ABOUT YOU
Products don't win for you. Concepts don't win for you. Systems don't win for you. Image doesn't win for you. Advertising doesn't win for you… YOU WIN FOR YOU.
- You make the difference
- Whether you are a stud or dud, accept responsibility for your life
- Life is the biggest of leagues and time is running out
- On your tombstone will be written here is a dud or here is a stud
- To change, you've got to do something different. If you don't, the next 10-20 years will be a rerun.
- People buy YOU

EVEN THE COMPETITION SAYS ABOUT ME…
- He ain't no pansy
- He isn't a fence sitter
- ALW takes a position and so should you

THE WINNING EDGE
Mental toughness is the winning edge
- Most everyone in America says the right thing
- There is no other way to win other than to be a competitor, to compete
- Most of you spend your whole adult life taking it, and taking it, and taking it, and taking it
- Most people's peak years in their life are their high school and college years, when they are competing and feel special and are idealistic. But they graduate and people start tattooing them.
- The once vibrant person becomes a shell of a man, "life has just passed me by" is what they're thinking

TO BE ANYTHING YOU NEED TO HAVE...
- Desire. Desire is everything.
- No one has ever been able to design a test to look inside the heart of a man or a woman
- You can change your life in 30 days

Sugar Ray Leonard: "The toughest critic is the man in the mirror. You can lie to everybody else but yourself."

ART: "CHARGE"
- I made it because I had a big dream. I had a dream of $300,000 net worth. At 10% that amount would bring me $30,000 a year income for life
- I wanted to be my own man
- There's nothing like winning, like being somebody, like competing. Life is a series of challenges.
- The measure of a man is when things are all going bad, your best man quits, sales fall off, you hear negative comments and you keep charging
- In a hopeless situation always CHARGE
- If you really knew you can make $100,000 a year you wouldn't care what you were selling

ADVERSITY
- The enemy can't win: General George Patton... "The Germans are picking up their dead in horse drawn wagons because they don't have any gas".
- Two experiences you should have before your first sale...
  - The first 5 to 6 people say no
  - Imagine paying a death claim from your next appointment

CRUSADERS DIE HARD
- We are Crusaders
- We are on a mission out there because this is a worthwhile cause
- If the competition likes us we are in trouble
- We've got to get into the competing mode
- The greatest thing we've got going is that we sell term insurance
- The harder they attack us the more money we make. Competition is good for everybody.
- The enemy can't win because they don't do what's right for the consumer
- Term insurance is right
- The consumer picks up the cost for advertising and for new agents
- They are strong on image but weak at the kitchen table

THE AMERICAN PEOPLE WILL NOT FOLLOW
- a pansy
- a fence sitter
- a mealy mouth

People want to follow someone who is strong and takes a position. To be that you've got to be controversial.

- This is a company with a heart and with a philosophy
- We have a mission and a cause
- We have an intense loyalty and commitment to what we are all about. We are crusaders.
- Life will give you what you fight for

Call me anything but average an ordinary. If you accept average and ordinary and unhappiness, that's what life will give you.

- You can change your life in 30 days
- The first two years all I heard was no, no, no, then I paid a death claim and it changed my life forever
- I thought this works, this is for real, this is important. I had forgotten how many customers I had helped.
- All you can do is all you can do. It is impossible to do anymore.
- I owned term insurance, I did the best job for them, and they still said no.

Keep telling your story, keep telling your story, keep telling your story. Don't quit.

- If they didn't buy I thought to myself, "Of all the policies I've ever analyzed, yours was the worst, but it was just right for you."
- When they said to me, "No I don't want to work with you". I said to myself "Art you're such a dud."
- Existing licensed insurance agents are prima-donnas. They aren't tough enough. That's why you recruit greenies.

7/30/1988

ANGELA WILLIAMS

EFFORT AND ATTITUDE ARE UNDERVALUED
- Don't major in minor things
- Art is a proven example of wanting to be the best you can be.
- I love life: I love this business.
- We came into the business to be a crusader
- People around us deserve and need our great effort and attitude.
- ART wants unity. Any crisis binds us together and we've had plenty.
- I'm proud of this "be good or be gone "attitude

ART'S THOUGHTS
- If I'm not great, I should be gone and not embarrass myself
- Greatness requires leadership
- We are here to win or lose but not to just survive
- *We have to take people to places they don't want to be before they get to where they want to be*
- We need to make them feel uncomfortable to grow
- If we're not making changes we are in trouble
- Change, growth, monumental gutsy leaders are required to win and conquer the world

7/30/1988
FORT MYERS, FL
SNSD MEETING - INNER CIRCLE

OUR THEME: THE YEAR OF DECISIONS, ALW DECISIONS
Decisions to be a great company requires awesome decisions
1988 is the time to make your decision. The decision to increase your wealth by 4 to 5 times

MAKE A DECISION
- A decision to win or fade away
- A decision for greatness or a decision to lose
- A decision to be a success or be a has-been
- A decision to Be Somebody or be a nobody
- A decision to be a starter or be a bench player

- ALW has to cut some weak, dead limbs off to prune the system. To get rid of those who quit.

Ability doesn't win in ALW. It's effort and attitude!

- Those who have delivered haven't quit
- Keep fighting. Take advantage of our multiplication system.

BE GOOD OR BE GONE
- ALW is a company of destiny
- ALW fought many wars: the competition, the Better Business Bureau, financial scares, administration, the news media, politicians, persistency, leadership.
- ALW has the will to win
- ALW has the desire to win

WE WON BECAUSE THERE WERE NO OPTIONS
- There was not a business reason to believe we could win
- The only people not making it here are the dead butts
- We are a proud battle proven company

A little bit more is the winning edge.
The will to win is the winning edge.

A.L.WILLIAMS IS A SLEEPING GIANT WHO IS GOING TO SET RECORDS AND CREATE MILLIONAIRES
- What are you going to do?
- What part are you going to play?
- What kind of leader are you going to be?
- How bad do you want it?
- *The ones who don't make it are those who get too comfortable with life as it is*

STANDARDS OF EXCELLENCE
- With awesome standards you get an awesome paycheck. With low standards you get a low paycheck.
- If you think you're going to be financially independent with low standards you're wrong
- Be the best you can be in life, not just in our company
- Do you have a welfare mentality?

Most people can stay excited for one month, or one day, but a winner stays excited for as long as it takes to get the job done.

- Don't ever blame the company. Look in the mirror. Others are winning and you can too.
- We spend all our time justifying things to a deadbeat. Don't do it.

- For your production in the past that creates your income for the rest of your life, we have delivered for you

I expect you to be as great as you can be!

8/1/1988

MENTAL TOUGHNESS
- It's about WINNING or Losing
- Just don't quit. What about you? Are you a quitter? Quitters don't win and winners don't quit.
- Attitude and effort are most important
- ALW is a sleeping giant and so are you

THE WINNING EDGE IS
- Mental toughness
- Vision and determination that create the thrill of a fight
- The feeling of accomplishment
- The challenge of adversity and still having the drive to win
- Having an organization of destiny
- Explosive
- An attitude to let it rip and get after it. A balls to the wall spirit and effort.

8/2/1988

ATTITUDE, BELIEF, EXAMPLE
- If you want to Be Somebody, this is the place to be
- It's an 8 to 10 year period of sacrificing now to become stone wealthy later
- Have an "All you can do is all you can do" attitude
- Be an example
- Believe in the system. Believe in the opportunity
- You win by doing the right kind of things consistently

The way to recruit a Larry Weidel or Mike Tuttle is to recruit 100's of people.

If you let it rip, let it all hang out, I promise you that you will win.

THIS IS A NUMBERS BUSINESS
- People quit just before they make it
- The darkest days of life are just before you make it big
- It takes 3 to 5 years to establish yourself in the business
- If you lose a great guy, don't worry about it
- "The other guy will quit or slow down but not me" has to be your attitude
- 95% of the plays you call won't work, but some will
- 95% of the time you feel like the business isn't working like it should. But it will.
- Teams that win fight and play hard for 4 quarters. They believe each play called will win the game.
- You can't ever give up
- Every game lasts 4 quarters so assume the fourth quarter is when it all comes together
- Fight until you win
- Recruit somebody, look at them as a stud, love them, meet their spouse and drive it down 4 deep quickly. Yet 95% of them won't work out.
- You don't have to be great in sales, or in recruiting, and be successful to become wealthy. You just have to keep showing up to fight
- Some years your income will go down
- Arts best coaching year is when he had a losing record: three wins and seven losses, but he kept working.
- You can't feel sorry for yourself
- Those who win have intensity, the will to win and they keep trucking
- You are one recruit away from an explosion
- You win with the fundamentals
- It's a blessing to have to make 15 sales just to earn $3000 a month.
- It takes years of working through the hard times to learn the fundamentals and to fight through the hard times
- It's impossible not to be financially independent if you give all you got for 8 to 10 years
- Where else are we going to go for people like me and you to have a chance to be wealthy?
- Give it all you have for 4 quarters and you will win

TAKE OWNERSHIP
- You achieve another level of success when you start looking at this as your business
- Take it personally, internalize it, own it
- You will have the pride and love of ownership that will propel you

8/3/1988
NAPLES, FL

- The Computer doesn't discriminate
- When things are bad you don't need hearts and flowers, you need honesty and courage

ANGELA WILLIAMS

- Be tough enough to take Art's discipline as a coach
- We can all be negatively influenced. You are influenced by those you associate with.
- From the heart springs all kinds of evil. Have the right heart.
- Real Crusaders don't care and it doesn't matter
- Have the right faith in Art and Boe
- Trust in the Lord: You honestly can't trust any leaders even if they're good. Because God has all the control
- God will give you the desires of your heart. Trust in your heart that He is in control.
- Therefore, be able to have faith in leaders and in yourself
- Never do anything for short-term results or short term pleasures

8/8/1988
RITZ CARLTON

1988 – The year of decisions. A.L. Williams has made a decision. The decision is to be a great company.

DECIDE THAT YOU WILL...

- Be a great organization. That you are an organization of destiny.
- That you will lead an historical organization
- That you will make big money; millions of dollars a year
- That you will sell a high quality of life
- That you will get yourself into a position to quadruple your wealth
- Do something special with your life
- Change the lives of millions of people
- Build incredible wealth
- Build something you are proud of
- Do something truly magnificent
- Capitalize on your years of strain and effort
- Take advantage of the years of sacrifices you've made
- Be proud
- Realize all the bad stuff you've been through to get where you are which allows you to do something great in the future

MAKE A DECISION TO NEVER...
- Fade away
- Be a has-been
- Be a nobody
- Be a non-factor
- Become frustrated and bitter

YOUR JOB
Find the 11 best people to be your starters. Find those that don't want it and put them on the bench.

9/19/1988

THE PRICE OF WINNING
- Must know in your gut how badly you want to win
- One thing all winners have is an unbelievable desire to Be Somebody so bad that it won't let you rest
- Companies don't win for you, products don't win for you. It's you!
- How tough are you?
- How much do you believe?
- When you're hurting, how tough are you?
- When the competition comes, how tough are you?
- Do you have the will to win, the intensity, the mental toughness to win?
- You'll have nightmares for years to come if you don't win
- It'll haunt you for the rest of your life

Winners find a way to win.

PREPARATION FOR WINNING
- Are you prepared to not lose the edge, the excitement?
- Are you prepared to handle adversity?
- Are you really a winner when the tough times come? Or do you wimp out?
- Are you prepared for people to avoid you?
- Are you prepared to stand for something?
- Are you prepared with the proper intensity it takes?
- Are you prepared and wanting to Be Somebody?

I LOVE THE FREE ENTERPRISE SYSTEM
I love the competition, the pressure to win, the fight, the controversy, the heartache and the success and wealth that it all brings.

I LOVE...
The BIG pressure, the big rewards, the big money, the big effort, the big success, the big stress, the big explosive income, the big frustration, the big recognition, the big people problems, the big travel, the big home, the big office problems, the big prestige, the big recruiting, the big security, the big sales, the big generation to generation income, the big chargebacks, the big prosperity.

ALW CREATED A SYSTEM
- That would give us a winning edge
- That system gives people:
    - A taste of freedom
    - A taste of opportunity
    - A taste of management
    - A taste of success

RECRUITING TIPS
We prospect by recruiting. We hire bird dogs but we don't treat them that way. It's just a way to understand our system of creating sales through a person's natural market.

10/16/1988
INNER-CIRCLE MEETING
ATLANTA, GA

THE COMPANY
The company is doing 70,000 life apps per month now

ALW IS MY LIFE
- I want to be part of a happening
- I feel a burden to deliver for our people and our clients.
- For the consumer because if not for ALW they would be lost
- We are something special in America.
- Some RVPs are not making it like they could
- I'd give a part of my income for them to make it
- The numbers can be misleading

- A percentage want to stay where they are. Do you want to play it safe or go for a home run?
- We have an opportunity to build an empire
- We are going to go for it, if not, we'd hate ourselves
- Leadership is everything. Leaders can change their environment.

10/17/1988

LEADERS
- Leaders are precious and rare. People are hungry for a leader. That's why they are attracted to you. They are starved for a leader.
- You get more out of your people with positive motivation
- People also need to know there is a downside
- Let your people know that through thick or thin you are going to be here for them
- Leaders tell people that most of them won't make it, but if they do it's worth it
- Leaders take a position
- Leaders are hated by 5% of the people they lead, but 95% love them
- Leader set goals for the team. Three years have 100,000 RLs with 1500 showcase offices in America
- ALW is the company that produces the most millionaires
- Leaders are strong when negative news comes down. They are rocks to their people.
- Leadership can make a difference
- They call the shots, have retreats, get togethers and spend money to move ahead
- Leaders want to explode not fizzle. Leaders would rather burn out than rust out
- Leaders realize the difference between themselves and those ahead of them is just time and compounding effort
- Leaders realize you can't teach a pig to sing
- Leaders understand the momentum that is upon us
- Leaders don't follow the BS of other companies that there is quicker or easier money to be made over there
- Leaders realize a big base shop and making money is the only way to get your people doing more.
- Are you one of the 98% of followers or are you a 2% of the leaders?
- Understand losers are negative
- Have a total, unconditional positive attitude
- Play hurt
- Are you committed to win?
- Give your people the freedom to determine their own destiny
- Leaders are not managers
- Capture the power curve of the MULTIPLES
- You will make mistakes because you are human
- Understand that your reputation is everything
- Leaders live on character and pride

- Leaders are thrilled by their people prospering
- Leaders face challenges, doubts, fears and depressions, but they keep on fighting
- Leaders have total faith in the company and its leaders and their decisions
- Leaders never lose sight of the objective
- Leaders realize that not everyone is going to make it big
- Leaders realize you win by producing big guys

WHO WILL MAKE IT IN ALW?
- People with desire and determination
- Find people with these ingredients and you've got some studs
- Leaders realize few people are willing to slop it up like we do
- I am a ball buster
- These are the kind of people who make it in this business
- Leaders deal with prospecting, competition, the uglies, and home office screwup's
- Leaders realize if they lay it on the line for 5–10 years, it will pay off for their families
- Leaders are willing to pay any kind of price to win
- Leaders want to Be Somebody
- Leaders realize everybody wants to Be Somebody
- Leaders don't believe in resurrecting the dead
- Leaders don't let the duds dominate their time
- Leaders are mad men, are fanatical, and are obsessed, or it seems like it

10/19/1988

WHY ARE PEOPLE FAILING?
No confidence in themselves and are hurt by people who are putting them and our system down.
Someone needs to believe in them. Leaders can make a difference by loving them the right way.
They don't understand what to do. We need to train and teach them.

- A leader is an example. People want to follow people who are real.
- You can make $100,000 a year, $1 million a year, $5 million a year here. Yes YOU!
- Leaders can make a difference. ALW is spending millions for you to develop leaders.

EXPECT YOUR PEOPLE TO WIN
- Don't give up on them, care about them, believe in them
- Have high standards
- The goal is having the desire to Be Somebody
- The goal is having a will to win
- The goal is having a big vision
- Build people through recognition and praise

11/23/1988
ART WILLIAMS ON ALW-TV

THE DREAM
- To go into business for yourself
- To control your own destiny
- To make and save money
- To Be Somebody
- To do something special with your life
- To produce other people like yourself - duplication
- To get something for nothing
- To build financial independence
- To do something for your family that gives them an edge in life
- To change your whole family, to break the cycle of financial MEDIOCRITY for them. Your family will elevate themselves because of you.

It's a shame to only build a base shop.

- The goal is to reach hundreds of thousands of people and motivate the world
- You own your own company; make yourself financially independent and build your company within a company
- Build 7–10 key leaders… Ball busters
- Have the Pride of Ownership
- Have a builders mentality

- Be proud of your people
- WIN for you and your family
- Leaders train the trainers
- People don't work just for money. Know what motivates people.

- Be a crusader
- In your heart know that what you are doing is right
- Prospect by recruiting
- Sales management is the best of sales and education
- In sales you are unemployed every day and have no security

- You don't have to be a superstar, you don't have to kill yourself here, but you must recruit
- You can take time off and the MULTIPLES will still happen

RVP AND THE MULTIPLES
Have a builders mentality.......
- Building $100,000 base shop is tough; you aren't good enough but you CAN get 10 RVPs.....
- @ $10,000 = $100,000
- 5 each = 50 @ 5,000 = $250k
- 5 each = 250 @ 5,000 = $1.25M
- What if you do 50% of that? 25% of that?

1/9/1989

No way corporate America will give the guy that looks like me, with my brain, a chance to get to the top. Our goal is to be known as a company that produces the most financially independent families.

TO WIN BIG
- Build 7-10 good people
- Builders are dreamers
- You be a head coach
- Surges are critical
- Sell out for 30 days
- Be totally excited
- Be totally committed
- Dreamers build hope

1/10/89

INNER CIRCLE CONFERENCE CALL

- I am blown away by the importance of ALW in making the families in America better
- I'm at peace with my life
- I want ALW to pay off for our precious families, who made a commitment to us for 8–10 years
- Leadership is everything
- ALW is built for you and your family to win
- Focus on your business and make your own individual organizational goals

- Don't get lost with all the Mickey Mouse, nonsense things that happen to you along the way, because they will happen

5/1/1989

THE MAGIC AND POWER...
- The difference between building a team and building your business is how you treat your people
- Sincerely love and care about people. Build personal relationships
- There is a special magic and power in building relationships
- There is a magic and power in you building a business family
- A special power and magic in the crusade; it gives you the edge
- A special power and magic in the changing of people's lives, as coaches do
- A special magic and power in looking for the good things in people
- A special magic and power in building friendships
- A special power and magic and having fun in the business
- A special power and magic in togetherness, collectively accomplishing something great
- A special power and magic in offering families a special chance to build financial independence and security
- A special power and magic in financial independence and security through overrides and not sales. Overrides are secure and stable.
- A special power and magic in seeing people feel good about themselves
- A special power and magic and love for the ALW company, its people, its customers, and what the crusade brings
- A special power and magic in the multiples

7-10 RVPS - THE POWER OF THE MULTIPLES
- One day seems like a year in ALW, it's tough and lonely out there
- There's power and magic in the numbers
- To be wealthy you must have a 7–10 key RVPs with everyone doing a little bit
- When we all do it collectively, you build your fortune
- 7 RVPs who gets 7 RVPs who get 7 RVPs = 139,000 RVPs
  - Or 5 RVPs @ 5 RVPs each = 19,530 RVPs
  - 1 RVP @ $5,000 and they do thru 6 = $48,000 year
  - or 2 = $14,000 a month
  - or 3 = $71,000 a month
  - or 4 = $360,000 a month
  - or 5 = $1,000,000 a month
  - or 6 = $2.9M a month
  - or 7 = $7M a month, $84M a year

POWER AND MAGIC IN THE MULTIPLES
You don't think the multiples can happen to you but they will happen, if you don't quit

DUMB ASSES
People who don't seem to understand the magnitude of what we are doing. They are dumb asses.
- They are people who never built anything
- They are people who try to build something but can't get along with other people

THE MULTIPLES
The Key: HUGE NUMBERS OF PEOPLE = A Huge Organization
- The multiples won't happen if you:
  - Quit or if you stop producing new people
  - If you stop selling a dream, vision and mission
  - These are the reasons the multiples stop
- The multiples start with just one recruit

DEVELOP 7–10 KEY RVPs AND KEY PEOPLE
- How? By loving them and caring about them
- Jesus started with only 12 special people

CHARACTERISTICS OF SPECIAL PEOPLE
- They are good students of the business
- They want to know they are not hurting people
- They recruit people that love people
- They are producers and not talkers or benchwarmers
- They produce what they have to produce to survive by making sales and making money
- They have a supportive spouse

2 THINGS REQUIRED TO MAKE IT BIG
1. Work hard   2. Don't quit

5/15/89

- You can't take a dud and make them a stud no matter how much you care for them
- Loser thinking - you'd be crazy to join ALW because it's nasty, hard and you have to pay a terrible price. There is always a price in winning.

Most of you aren't tough enough. But like in football, we let you put on the jockstrap and see what you can do.

- The key is not how you look/talk, but your desire and will to win
- The studs are the producers

MILLIONAIRES
- No company has produced more millionaires than ALW
- ALW will fight for you
- ALW are mavericks, weirdos, people who have a warped sense of destiny
- They want to be different and revel in being different

IT'S US AGAINST THEM
- Elitists put us down
- They say something is wrong with ALW because of the people we build it with
- They think we are cornball and we fell off the back of a turnip truck

ALW VERSUS MLM
- Our opportunity to make money is real
- They over-promote their opportunity
- No one ever makes money with them
- They over-promote what their product can do while our products deliver death claims
- They have no crusade, they razzle and dazzle you with circles
- At ALW the crusade is our life
- This is a search and destroy mission. We are not to looking to coexist but to eradicate the competition from the face of the earth.
- ALW is cause driven
- MLM is quick saturation

WHY DO I GET SO EMOTIONAL?
- Because ALW is my life
- If you have any honor, integrity, character and you are attacked you don't wimp out and run away from the fight
- This is something worth believing in and fighting for
- I've dedicated my life to ALW and its people
- People will remember me or not remember me, based upon what I've done in ALW
- "What they're doing is screwing people." I hate whole life insurance companies
- ALW is not perfect but compare us to something else out there. We are the best.

LEADERSHIP
- Put people ahead of yourself
- Look for the good things in people
- A leader has a giving heart and a caring spirit
- Inch by inch it's a cinch by the yard it's hard
- Make 8 X 10 monthly your commitment

6/5/1989

CONQUER THE WORLD
- You sell out to winning
- Let's make a blood pact together to win
- We can conquer the world together
- You can't do it alone. It's called team spirit.
- Without a big dream you are dead
- The dream fuels desire
- See yourself as an......
    - RVP
    - SVP
    - NSD
    - SNSD
    - Building a national company
    - Building RVPs
- To make it happen, sell out to your dream
- Recommit now to sell out to the dream

WHAT CAN WEAR YOU DOWN?
- Problems
- Negative people
- Putting out fires

CREATE A POSITIVE ATMOSPHERE
- I don't care how impossible it looks, we are going to win
- I'm going to Be Somebody
- Winners burn all their bridges and sell out
- You can only build financial independence with a team
- I'm the head coach
- Sell a dream of financial independence and owning your own company
- Challenge them one more time
- Believe in them one more time
- Sell a vision of greatness and hopefulness
- Keep selling a vision of greatness and hope until you die

WHAT CAN CAUSE YOU TO LEVEL OFF?
- Individual concept
- Individual mentality
- Not a team concept
- We, our, us, and we can conquer the world
- We draw off each other's strength, energy, and success

THINGS TO WORK ON FOR 30 DAYS
- Be a head coach that cares. You can't show hurt or quit.
- Identify a vision of greatness as an NSD and SNSD
- Have a longterm vision to be big and conquer the world, like Bob Buisson
- Build your own national company
- Have a crusade that gives you the extra ounce of courage, confidence and pride
- Challenge each individual to do what they can for the next 30 days. Go to your next promotion level.
- Have an atmosphere of tremendous excitement
- Spend time with those who want it
- Identify potential superstars and find your 7–10 key people
- Do it inch by inch
- Sell out to greatness through recruiting
- Keep expanding the vision to your team. Keep expanding your dreams and visions
- Don't quit until you die and don't show hurt
- Keep yourself liquid
- Show emotion by showing that you cry, you hug, and tell them they are special
- Our top priority is to keep winning

LIVE AND DIE
- Live and die with recruiting
- Live and die with promotions
- Live and die with big events

7/10/89

BE SOMEBODY
This is my one chance to Be Somebody and build a company. I may not have another.
- No one will deny me this opportunity to Be Somebody
- Now it is my time to put it in the end zone

7/24/1989

DO THESE SIX THINGS TO EARN A SPOT ON THE FIRST TEAM
1. Unbelievably loyal to ART and to the company's decisions; enthusiastically endorse them
2. It's not good enough to have just a positive attitude, you must also have the ability to show it
3. Be tremendously creative by calling a shot when you need to call the shot
4. Super intensity
5. You can't have people on the first team every time. Just look at your income to see if you are a first teamer.
6. ALW has become a job to a lot of people. It's a LIFE not a job

- ALW wants to plow new ground and have phenomenal success

8/7/1989

TO WIN
- Are you ready to win for you and your family?
- The key to your future is you
- Have an unbelievable desire to Be Somebody
- I'm proud of the fight you fought
- Have good feelings about yourself
- Understand that nothing good comes easy
- You were born to be great – You were born to be special
- Everything in sales came hard for me

WHY PEOPLE FAIL
- Time runs out on them
- It takes 8–10 years to eventually make it BIG. This is not a get rich quick scheme.
- To win you need to change your life and take charge of your future

HISTORY TELLS US
- What works and doesn't work in building a business
- In 1977 ALW was formed to give everyone a chance to win
- You can't doubt the ALW system. We are winning
- Religiously working and recruiting makes you win
- Intensity of your effort and belief pays off
- It takes 9 to 10 years of work to build a lifetime income

HOW TO BUILD IT
1. Build a business; you have a chance to build one here
   - No matter what the obstacles, work, don't wait for it to get better
   - Do not wish your life away. Get to work on your dreams.
   - They keep building, keep promoting no matter how tough it gets
2. Understand ALW:
   - It's not a personal producing organization. We pay builders.
3. Overrides are the Gold Mine
   - Get obsessed until you get a person to RVP. You can't rest until then.
4. Build with the right kind of people
   - Not with insurance licensed people
   - We give you an opportunity to mess up
   - Build with greenies, not professional sales people
   - Salesmen have no friends
   - They have bad habits in sales and they are hard closers
   - Greenies: You hire better quality with greenies (no license, no experience)
5. Learn to build with referrals, don't cold call or use mailers
   - The best referral system is a new recruit
   - Best way to learn sales
6. Learn how to build momentum
   - Do things in bunches
   - Sell, recruit, promote in bunches
   - Use big meetings
7. Understand and teach REPLACEMENT:
   - Like exchanging your personal sale
   - Sell it upfront
   - We give people like us a chance to build it big because of replacement
8. Have a goal of greatness:
   - Have specific dreams. Have specific reasons.
   - I wanted to quit every day
   - What kept me going? My goal of greatness
9. To Win in this business you must understand the numbers
   - The numbers work
   - All you have to have is 7–10 RVPs

BUILDING A FEW KEY PEOPLE BUILDS WEALTH
- Build 7–10 key people to greatness
- Help 7–10 people, you build these 7–10
- Keep selling this vision and dream
- Keep building first generation RVPs and getting wide

- Your first RVP is the toughest
- Believe you are always one recruit away from a surge

KEY SKILLS
- Build and maintain a base shop
- Build quality first generation RVPs
- Become a motivator and a coach
- Understand the spread in this business
- Get wide, lock in deep, cash flow $100,000 a year in override income
- You want to personally produce until you cash flow $100,000 in override income
- You grow in plateaus
- You have to have local success. That person ought to be you
- I want my people to recruit like I recruit
- I want my people to make money like I make money
- You can't be motivated by the money first
- Love people and genuinely care about making them wealthy
- Look for the good things in people
- Become a leader. Leaders are made not born

THE TALENTS OF GREAT LEADERS
- They are super hard workers
- They don't quit
- They do it first and they have the mentality to do it first
- They believe they will find a stud someday soon
- They are great role models for their company
- They compete but don't compare
- They do a little bit extra one more time.
- They have the right kind of attitude about life
- They have the ability to show a great attitude
- They are positive, excited, enthusiastic and happy people
- They always pass positives down
- They sell the dream one more time
- They are pros and perform like pros
- They recognize people
- They praise their people
- They start winning with their family

GET EMOTIONAL
- Competition is a way of life in our business
- Always sell the dream
- Everybody wants to Be Somebody
- Duds sometime turn out to be studs and studs sometimes turn out to be duds

**8/10/1989
INNER-CIRCLE MEETING
NEW YORK, NY**

THE MAGNITUDE OF ALW
- We are going to make thousands of people financially independent
- Many will become incredibly wealthy
- Some will participate in this historic event

IF YOU DOUBT ALW
- Look at the excitement of a new recruit
- Look at the excitement of a new RVP

UNWRITTEN LAW - Keep people coming and keep people going.

9/25/1989

TO WIN YOU MUST BE
- Tough
- Dedicated
- Sold out
- Committed to win; not just show up

OUR FUTURE
- We have a chance to build another Coca-Cola.
- The only remaining challenge in ALW is a personal challenge of yours

WE BUILD PEOPLE, NOT... Premium, Sales, Wealth, Recruits.

10/2/1989

INTENSITY
- Be intense and excited about recruiting and YOUR LIFE
- Be constantly challenging your people to new heights by selling the dream
- Put points on the scoreboard in your life not just your business by winning in all areas
- Get a commitment from your people to get the ball in the end zone
- Be intense about Financial Independence, Recruiting, having RVPs
- Go RVP, SVP, NSD, SNSD
- Be totally financially independent
- Earning $100,000 a year override income

10/23/89

Concentrate on the power of the sizzle...Sell the sizzle and have the ability to transmit it.

HOW YOU SELL THE SIZZLE
- Tell war stories of people who have been successful
- Talk about the death claims we pay
- Have stories about improved lives of clients
- How our clients had a $50,000 policy and we gave them $300,000 of insurance for the same money
- Sell the local success potential of their city and that someone ought to be them to do it
- Talk about people that were making $38,000 a year in a job and are now making $500,000 a year
- Be a crusader because it will give you passion that OOZES out
- Believe intensely in what you are doing
- Be sold out to what you are doing
- Have the attitude: "I'm going to make it. I'm going to make every sale. I'm going to recruit every person"
- Always be attacking
- People buy you
- This is a numbers business. If the numbers work, and they do, the business works
- Be the best you can be
- Do things in surges by doing a lot over a short period of time

11/5/89
SANDY WEIL BUYS ALW

- We have a chance to make corporate history
- This is a new beginning
- Failure couldn't be considered because there was nothing to go back to
- This is a new company and a new era

ALW WAS BORN...
- Out of dreams
- In a commitment
- For a chance and a hope
- Without a contract or a guarantee
- Out of conviction
- Out of controversy
- Out of pride

- For a victory over the whole life industry
- For victory over the insurance commissioners
- For victory over banks
- For victory over The Better Business Bureaus and the National Life Underwriters Association
- For victory over home office problems
- For victory over newspaper attacks
- For victory over politicians
- For victory over persistency problems
- For victory over personal tragedies
- For victory over the death of some of our great leaders
- For victory over doubt and fear
- History was made and you were part of it

THE NEW ALW
We are participating in history. A new era of promotions. We are in an era of final permanency.
- This demands sacrifice
- Rewards will be bigger. Rewards will be quicker.

WE BROKE THE CODE IN FINANCIAL SERVICES
- I want to think BIG. To prosper and to win.
- This is not hype, this is for real

- Families like us want to make and accumulate wealth
- Don't worry about making mistakes
- Put points on the scoreboard
- It's time to light it up and go for it
- Experiment for a better future
- Stop thinking, analyzing, questioning, and figuring it out
- Be an action person
- We are here for your freedom
- You can be all you can think of being here at the company
- Promote people and make money

RESPONSIBILITY
Your responsibility here is to win
- To make money, save money, and be an example of success
- The difference between losing and winning is just a small fraction

WINNERS
- Winners or not born, are not talented, are not great speakers, or accomplished people
- Winners come from sheer effort and the desire to Be Somebody with an intensity that borders on fanatical

- Are balls-to-the-wall people. Take no prisoners

We might not make it if our leaders get satisfied.

WHY WE ARE WINNNG AND BUILDING A GREAT COMPANY
- Our concept is right. The consumer is right and must be served. We have right on our side.
- Our uniqueness is correct 100% of the time
- Money; People can make money here
- Product: Our customer satisfaction is high
- Commission: Renewals have been moved up to upfront cash
- Market; we have no competition
- Support administration is fantastic
- Commitment from a solid, major company to us. We are now part of the giant, Primerica.
- We have security for the first time in our history
- Our opportunity is now open ended

AT ALW WE PLEDGE OPPORTUNITY
But you can't take a dud and make them a stud

THEN... THE OLD DAYS BEFORE ALW
- It was hard to survive long enough to get a promotion
- It took 4-5 years to get to a secure override position
- It was hard to make big money
- We only had two choices: Take 8–10 years to get promoted or die along the way
- You could not build a company within a company

NOW... AT ALW
- You get promoted as early as you want
- You see success earlier
- You have more overrides and can own your own business quicker
- It's hard not to make $50,000 a year
- You make big money from a big base shop
- And the best is yet to come

OUR NUMBER ONE CHALLENGE
- To get RVP's income up
- Manage incomes
- Its feast or famine incomes
- Put the ball in the end zone or you get zero points
- This business is about making money
- The way to keep score is by how much money you are making.
- I'm all about winning

- It is not all bad to struggle, suffer or sacrifice to reach your dream

A GOOD RVP
- Is a good person and has a good family
- Has integrity
- Has mastered the art of praising people
- Is a good producer and produces recruits, sales, and promotions.
- It takes courage and compassion to sit with a starving RVP and tell him he is the reason.
- You double down your recruiting when you want a surge

- Life will not give you what you want, it gives you what you are willing to fight for
- All you can do for your people is be an example
- Your goal is to win for your family. It is the main focus of your business life.

Fight for those that want it. It's easy to quit with the losers, doubters and quitters.

- If any of you want to quit, go, but I'm staying to fight
- Build 7–10 key RVP's to win
- Don't quit until you are financially independent and stone wealthy

CONTRIBUTION
- My greatest contribution is giving you a chance to be a head coach
- My greatest contribution is giving you total freedom to build your business the way you want to

11/6/1989
PALM SPRINGS, CA

- The way to inspire old folks is to have new blood coming in constantly. New people bring excitement.
- Correctly Think because a great attitude is when our hearts and thinking are correct
- Compete by desiring to knock off the competition
- To win keep studying the business and keep trying to win

- Look for the little edges to get better by sharpening your focus on your goals

- We are in the promotion business. Keep people moving up the promotion system
- We are motivators and leaders, not insurance salesman
- In ALW you need an enemy, a critic, a devil's advocate who will give you the strength to win

- Believe we are an organization of destiny and are conquering the world
- Believe that we can become another Coca-Cola. Believe that we are going to make history
- Expand your vision by wanting to have offices in every major city
- Conquer the world

- At ALW everybody wants to be rewarded
- The winners prove themselves from Monday through Friday
- People are hungry for success. They truly want to Be Somebody but only one company will let them. That's this company
- If we all got totally focused and totally intense, imagine what we could do.

11/20/89

WE CAN BUILD AN EMPIRE WITH 400-500 FOCUSED PEOPLE

- The role of a coach is to kick butt
- ALW is an opportunity but not with a phony kind of prestige
- The person makes a position, a position does not make the person
- Every person wants to Be Somebody but their attitudes go sour because life beats them up
- You win Monday through Friday on the practice field
- The practice field is prospecting, selling and recruiting

WHAT IS THE PRICE OF WINNING?
- Selling something? Who wants to sell something, especially life insurance?
- Rejection? Know that it's a numbers business
- Make money and save money, pay the price! Make the money, don't spend it, keep your eye on the goal of financial independence
- I wanted to go out and get a good job every day. In-spite of the rejection and heartache, I kept working, earning money and saving. Financial independence was so precious to me.
- I wanted what only a hard price could get me
- Work hard
- Don't quit, ever

- Most plays don't work. In the real world 90% of things don't work out.
- Right Attitude: it's the next guy, the next person I talk to, it's the next person I call, that will make it all happen
- Competition is your ability to be motivated, to Be Somebody

DO IT
- Keep at it until you are earning $8,000 a month in overrides
- Work four nights a week and Saturday – Two presentations per night
- Get 5 FNAs a week

MINIMUM GOALS
- Have a $10,000 base
- Get 10 recruits a month
- Have 8–10 active recruits direct to you at all times.

WINNERS: They DO IT first

- You can change your life in 30 days
- Build 7–10 RVPs
- Get your base going to make the multiples happen
- Getting the first RVP is the toughest
- Build 4 deep

LAW: EVERYONE WANTS to make something off of someone else, called OVERRIDES.

A GROWING RVP
- Be a $50,000 earner and within three years produce an RVP who also earns $50,000 a year until you cash flow $8,000 a month. Be in the field 4 nights a week field training, have two presentations a night.
- Get one personal new recruit a week
- Do 5 FNAs a week
- Make three sales a week
- Keep the blinders on and never quit

WINNING GOALS:
- Maintain a $10,000 base
- Be involved in 10 base recruits a month
- Always have 10 direct legs to you at all times

WHAT TO BE GREAT AT
- Being a stud in the field training and recruiting
- 90% of the time field training in the field, recruiting, prospecting, selling and getting referrals
- Become a recruiting mad man
- Recruiting is the easiest way to prospect
- Create momentum by going wide
- Do things in surges
- Get good at getting commitments
- Treat people good
- Master the art of praise
- Master the art of recognition
- Be a winning example, be successful in your personal life, have a balanced life, live below your means
- Build Crusaders because reputation is everything
- Produce good quality business by always having a mutual fund sale with every insurance sale
- To get quality of business you need a large quantity of recruits; this is a numbers business
- Compete, don't compare, because jealousy and envy are your enemy
- Be proud by getting better every month
- Give your efforts time to compound
- The first 3–5 years are a roller coaster
- It takes 8–10 years to win
- Have a big dream of being financially independent
- Do things with a positive, happy and excited attitude
- Have a winning attitude
- Be someone who sells hope, dream and the opportunity

11/27/1989

I know that if I'm going to be big, I've got to do what others won't do.

MY HEROES WERE...
- Passionate about their business
- Heroes come from dreams and dedication

RECRUITING
- 1 Recruit brings 25 names
- You will see 10 of those recruits yield 8 sales

THE POWER OF ONE RECRUIT
- Recruit 4, get 16 by going 4 deep
- Recruit 25, get 100 by going 4 deep

1/8/1990

WHY DON'T NATIONAL CHAMPIONS REPEAT
- They get satisfied and comfortable
- They lose an ounce of intensity and courage, then it's all over

TO WIN
- Only work with people that want it
- Don't listen to the Duds
- Build a whole new wave of great leaders

A DUD
A Non-NSD who does less than $2,000 a month

The slogan in the LA Lakers locker room: "Somewhere, someplace sometime you are going to have to plant your feet, make a stand and kick some ass. And when that time comes, you do it."

AN ICONS CREED
Almost everybody can stay motivated for 2 to 3 months but a winner stays motivated for as long as it takes to get the job done

WHAT YOU MUST DO PERSONALLY TO MAKE YOURSELF A STUD
- Get excited, be happy, be positive, be on fire and show it.
- Become a leader: Do it first; say "watch me"
- Be a good person, look for ways to praise people, look for something to praise people about
- Catch people in the act of doing something right
- The winner in everybody's eyes is a fighter.

BEING SOMEBODY
- Being somebody! What is it? Look in the mirror and say "I was all right. I fought a good fight. I did something I didn't think I could do."
- When your wife or husband looks at you and is proud and glad that they have you
- Your grandkids look at you as a stud and are thankful that they've got your blood

- I didn't like Art. I was tired of having regrets. Tired of never having gone for it and laying it on the line.
- I never let it all out. I was going to do something one time in my life. One time in my life I could say I tried, that I let it all out, that I gave it my best.

- I pitched my tent
- Don't let fear keep you from teeing it up and winning
- Don't wimp out, don't throw in the towel and don't quit on you
- If you've never been what you want to be, go lay it on the line and see the miracles that will happen

FUNDAMENTAL LAWS
- Don't listen to anyone but the studs who are doing it. There is nothing you can do to revive the duds.
- Don't listen to the duds but rather sell the dream to them, before they unload
- Motivate them, sell the dream again and again
- Build a whole new generation of leaders. Keep the new ones coming in.

1/22/1990

- Are you willing to fail long enough until you win? Are you willing to fail over and over and over again until you experience the dream?

Failing is a part of winning. But failures can never win... because they quit.

- The main thing is to keep the "main thing", the main thing
- You have to survive long enough to taste victory at the end
- You churn, you burn, and send out sparks. Where the spark hits, another fire begins.
- You can control only two things: your attitude and your activity

2/12/1990

PLAY GOOD OFFENSE AND DEFENSE
- You do it
- You put your name on applications
- You recruit 5 direct people a month
- You write combination sales (life plus mutual funds)
- You have an us against them attitude
- You get your spouse involved
- You make money, save money and wait two years to make any dramatic changes in your standard of living

HOW TO AVOID PANIC MANAGEMENT:
- Caused by lack of activity
- Not being wide enough
- Not remembering spread

- Get 7–10 wide and four deep. This creates a solid business.

1/15/1990

TO WIN
- Balls-to-the-wall effort
- Take no prisoners
- When you display these traits, your people will love it
- It takes a total commitment to do whatever it takes and whenever it takes to get the job done
- It's not talent, it's not brains… it's recruits
- Every skill we develop, we earn
- Sales, prospecting, speaking all scared the winners
- They had an incredible will to win, an intensity to win and they worked, worked, worked
- They hurt and doubted just like the losers, but they kept working and working
- The day you feel you're too good to have an appointment or be in the field, or recruit people, it's over
- Winners were desperate. They didn't know what they were doing, they just did it.
- How bad do you want it?
- You can't just fall into it
- People like us don't fall into anything but the bad stuff
- Are you fanatical?
- On your tombstone; Will it read "Here lies a dud" or "Here lies a stud"?
- You do it. You go Be Somebody you are proud of

Somewhere, someplace, sometime you'll have to come to the point where you have to plant your flag and kick some butt. When your time comes, you do it.

CHARGE!
The price: You come to a point where you have to make a decision, where it looks hopeless. When that happens you fight back. When that happens you kick some butt. Something hits you in the face and it looks hopeless.

It will happen to you. What will your response be?

When that moment arrives, when that moment of truth comes, when things haven't worked out, at that moment, when it's impossible, CHARGE!
- When it seems like you're dying, CHARGE!
- When you're hurting, CHARGE!

- When you're struggling, CHARGE!
- A winner can't show doubt

A COACHES RESPONSIBILITY
- Work with those who want it. You can't revive the dead. They have a bad attitude? Move on.
- Put the 11 best people on the field
- Show your team your best players
- At fast start schools don't let the good old guy speak
- Don't listen to or worry about the bitchers, the whiners, the complainers or the duds. Just don't let them dump on you.
- Constantly be building a whole new generation of leaders in your base

PRINCIPLES
- Get excited, happy and show it
- Be a leader, not a boss
- Say "watch me"
- Be a good person
- Be a winner. A winner produces.
- Be a fighter

ALWAYS...
- Surge: rethink your prospect list
- Raise expectations
- Promote the next big event
- Recognize big base shops again
- Remember, more recruits bring more code numbers

Art Williams: Part 8

"CRUSH YOU"

4/7/2007

ART WILLIAMS: PART 8
"CRUSH YOU"

4/7/07
HOUSTON, TX

*The recruit that will change your life will always come after some major disappointment that will almost **CRUSH YOU**.*

COMMITMENT
You need to make a 100% commitment to one thing, recruiting and building RVPs. We are not in the sales business.

CAPTURE THE SPIRIT TO KEEP THE MAGIC IN THE TEAM
Never forget the things that blew your butt out of the water the first time you saw this opportunity:
- The magic of compound interest
- The growing by multiplication
    - 3x3x3x3x3x3x3x3x3x3 = 59,000
- The power of your personal story. How you got into the business and what your life was like when you got in.
- Don't rely on tricks or gimmicks. All you need is a scratch pad and a pen.

HEART POWER
- Heart...You win with your heart not your head
- Heart power wins
- People fall in love with you, the company and the hope it brings
- Money and success will follow the heart

Vince Lombardi said "The secret of winning is heart power. If you capture a person's heart, you capture the person."

COACH TALK
- Are you tough enough?
- We sell hope and an opportunity
- Give people a chance to get the Friday night feeling back again. A chance to get excited again, to dream again and to make a difference with their lives

OWNERSHIP
- A rental car versus a car you own? Which do you take care of better?
- Ownership is all-powerful

- The free enterprise system allows you to go into business for yourself
- Everybody wants to own something, home or land or a business
- Never allow your people to think that they are working for you

RELATIONSHIPS
- Get involved in people's lives
- Get involved in their messes
- Get involved in their family and their dreams
- Tell them you love them
- Find a way to make people feel special
- The most powerful 4 words in the English language are "I believe in you".

I WANTED TO BE FINANCIALLY INDEPENDENT SO BAD THAT IT BECAME AN OBSESSION.

- Only 2% of the people in America are financially independent.

FINISH LINE
Never stop until you go through the finish line, no matter how many times you start

You beat 90% of the people by working hard, living right and finding something you can believe in. The top 10% is a dogfight.

- 90% of the people get tired and quit and that's when you beat them

DISCIPLINE is doing what you're supposed to do, when you are supposed to do it. Show up and work, whether or not you feel like it

SACRIFICE is giving up the things you want immediately to achieve your long range goals

BE A DREAMER AGAIN
- Like when you and your spouse were in high school dreaming about your future together
- When you graduated from school thinking about your life ahead
- Life can deal you a bad hand sometimes and you start to think you can't dream again
- ALW gives you a chance to dream again, hope again and be excited again
- We change lives

ENCOURAGE
The things that get praised get done. Look for the good things in people

THE IMPORTANCE OF YOUR SPOUSE
- Your spouse is the most important person in your business. A husband and wife together building a business is the most important part of your business.
- I need their encouragement, support, love and patience
- My role to my spouse is to make it big, to make money and save money, handle money wisely and to praise and encourage them constantly

BECOME A MOTIVATOR
Motivating is the role of a head coach. You must get emotionally involved with your people.

LEADERSHIP:

An army of deer led by a lion will defeat an army of lions led by a deer.

ATTITUDE
- Attitude is everything
- You need to work on your attitude daily
- The glass is always half full
- You can never say "I'll stick my toe in it, if it works, then I'll go whole hog"
- Jump in fully with total commitment
- "Things are never as good as they seem or as bad as they seem"
- You can't ever recruit enough people
- You can never make enough money
- You can never save enough money
- This is a roller coaster business that has its ups and downs

THE 2 WORST WORDS IN THE ENGLISH VOCABULARY -
"I CAN'T". *You can do anything if you want it badly enough.*

SELL THE BEST THING YOU'VE GOT - THE OPPORTUNITY.

COMMIT TO YOUR BUSINESS
- Commit to one thing
- As in a marriage, you need to commit to one person
- Be faithful to one person
- Be faithful to your one business

COURAGE IN THE FACE OF REJECTION
- The first 18 months everything I heard was "no"
- Rejection just about destroyed me but I kept going
- I didn't remember the yes's. I focused on the bad appointments. I had to fight through it. To change my mindset.
- When someone wanted to keep their whole life policy I thought "Of all the whole life I've ever seen, yours is the worst, but it is just perfect for you."

FAILURE
- 98% of the plays you call don't work. A team that wins believes that the plays they are calling will work.
- Look at everyone you recruit as an RVP
- Things will happen, just keep calling the plays

PANIC MANAGEMENT
- Lack of activity causes panic management
- Lack of money causes panic management
- Be a fanatic at controlling your expenses
- Never get into debt
- Never buy things that depreciate in value
- Don't loan money to your people
- Save money because one day you will need it if you have a disaster or an emergency
- Save money and one day money will save you
- Wait 90 days to buy things
- Be lean and mean financially

DO IT FIRST
Never ask your people to do something you are not willing to do

BE TOUGH
- Have a chip on your shoulder.
- Get a mad-on
- You can't show doubt, hurt or quit

Reward and punish yourself for either good or bad activity.

YOU DEVELOP FEELINGS AND INSTINCTS BY DOING IT
Rules, regulations and guidelines don't have a lot to do with success.

FAMILY
- We saw ALW as a family
- Make your people feel like they are part of your family
- Treat people like you treat your children

JUST DO IT
- "Almost" is a way of life for most people

4/16/2007
HOUSTON, TX

LEARN YOUR BUSINESS
- You learn this business by going through the tough stuff. There really isn't any way we can design our company to make it easier. We want to, but there isn't an easier way
- We change people's dreams, we change their hopes, ALW was more than just another company.

WHERE HAVE ALL THE GIANTS GONE?
- ALW wasn't a sales company. Sales are a byproduct. We are in business to give people a chance to build a business.
- To become a giant, you need to get out of the sales business
- You can't get your people thinking we are in sales. It will destroy your business.
- Sales teaches you how to prospect. We use the nine points system
- We don't teach people how to prospect strangers

TWO PEOPLE WHO ARE COMMITTED CAN CONQUER THE WORLD
- To win you commit to one thing. That one thing is to build a business. You must give everything you believe to that one thing.
- It's a belief system you don't change

SALES
- You are unemployed every day
- You have a limited opportunity to make money because there is just you

YOU NEED TO BUILD A TEAM
Building a team builds a secure income. Your income comes from hundreds and thousands of people. Building a team creates an unlimited income.

2% OF THE PEOPLE MAKE IT, PERIOD
- 16 out of 800
- They want to Be Somebody so bad it hurts
- They hang in there
- They have the heart to make it

DUD OR STUD
- What is your tombstone going to say about you? DUD or STUD?
- You can't fool the man in the mirror. Only you know whether or not you made it
- I can look in the mirror. I am proud of what I did and what I was a part of.

2%'ERS
- Are so self motivated it is ridiculous. 2%'ers are so focused it is ridiculous
- They constantly think that they're supposed to Be Somebody
- It's not talent, it's not education, it's not brains, it's wanting to Be Somebody so bad they can't stand it
- I couldn't stand the thought of my wife and kids thinking I'm a dud
- I couldn't recruit enough, make enough money, save enough money or promote enough RVPs.
- Nothing could stop me
- I am a madman
- How bad do you want to Be Somebody?

Crusade motivation 51%.
MONEY motivation 49%.

- ALW was born to bring the whole life industry to its knees
- Our mission is to give a different kind of person and opportunity to build a company within a company
- The kind of people with the heart, with the want-to and who desire to correct an injustice

COMMIT TO THE SYSTEM
Everyone commits to our system. Then you grow by multiplication

WHY BUILD A TEAM
Building a team allows average and ordinary people to do extraordinary things
- Recruiting is being obsessed with giving people hope and an opportunity
- Recruit good people, *not resumes or degrees*

HOW WE BUILT ALW
3x3x3x3x3x3x3x3x3... Do this and you will build an EMPIRE

GOALS
- Become an RVP
- Build 7–10 first generation RVPs
- Help your people build 7–10 RVP's each
- 7x7x7

HOW TO BUILD A TEAM
Have a simple system that everyone understands and can believe in

THINGS YOU DO
- Important: RECRUITING
- Unimportant: paperwork, being a manager
- Build an organization that can handle and promote big numbers
- This is a part-timer's company

HOW TO BUILD A SYSTEM THAT EVERYONE BELIEVES IN AND CAN FOLLOW THE ALW WAY
- Never talk to strangers. Never go to a strangers home
- Never see yourself in sales
- You can succeed by recruiting an endless number of prospects in the hot market
- Sales come through recruiting a friend with good credibility and you go see their best friends

SIMPLIFY WITH THE 9 POINT PLAN
1. Recruit a part-timer with a warm market
2. The part-timer sets up the appointment
3. The part-timer drives so you won't get lost
4. Go in the back door to the den or the kitchen
5. The new recruit acts as a cheerleader
6. No sale is made on the first interview because it's stupid
7. Recruit the friend
8. The friend sets up up an appointment with his best friend
9. Do this over and over and over and over

RECRUIT PEOPLE THAT HAVE A WARM MARKET
- Best friends
- Neighbors
- Work friends
- Kids parents
- School activities friends
- People in sports
- Family

BUILD A TEAM
To get 11 starters for a football team you need 1,100 kids to start peewee football. To get 11 $100,000 earners you need to recruit 1,100 people.

PEOPLE FAIL BECAUSE THEY DON'T RECRUIT ENOUGH
- It's mathematically impossible not to make it here
- 2%er's get 7-10 RVPs
- To get the multitudes you work the multiples
- 3x3x3x3

The multiples are the Ninth Wonder of the World

YOU ARE ONE RECRUIT AWAY FROM AN EXPLOSION.

YOU CAN SOLVE EVERY PROBLEM IN LIFE BY RECRUITING SOMEONE AND DRIVING THEM 4 DEEP.

- The power of the part-time concept is allowing people to build a company within a company

THE NEVERS OF THE ALW SYSTEM
- Never bring a best friend to an opportunity meeting first. Always do a one on one first at their home or at a coffee shop.
- Never have a new associate explain the business without a field trainer being with them
- Never sell on the first interview
- What does a new associate say to get an appointment? That's easy. What do you normally say to a friend?
- When does the sale happen? When it's supposed to.

SALE EXCHANGE SYSTEM
You can't make your own sale. The privilege of the right to work here is that you make the sale on each new recruit you get... SALES ARE A BYPRODUCT OF WHAT WE DO.

I HATE SALES.

I love A.L.WILLIAMS because we give people a chance to own their own business.

GET BIG
- Be prepared to conquer the world by opening offices all around the world
- By creating a new generation of big thinkers that love it like we do
- Important – it's important that you do work that you are proud of
- Always call the play. It's your life. You call the play and not wait for the coach to call the play

TO GO FULL TIME
- Have an emergency fund of $5,000 – $10,000
- Build a team to have overrides coming in
- Experience some of the ups and downs of the business before you go full-time

YOU CAN NEVER RECRUIT TOO MANY PEOPLE

PURPOSE OF AN OPPORTUNITY MEETING
- Never the first meeting for a new person
- To reinforce and cheerlead the system
- To bring emotion and passion to the opportunity
- To capture their hearts and hopes

Art Williams: Part 9

THE GREATNESS OF A.L. WILLIAMS

10/29/1996

ART WILLIAMS: PART 9
THE GREATNESS OF A.L.WILLIAMS

10/29/96

I can't understand why no one has copied the accomplishments of ALW.

OUR GREATNESS
- We built a different kind of company
- We built it with a different kind of people
- Not with businessmen or salespeople
- We built it with Crusaders and diehards
- We have a crusade
- We make a difference
- We stopped insurance companies from tattooing people
- We dedicated our lives to correcting an injustice
- We sold the pot at the end of the rainbow, the ALW dream
- The difference between winning and losing is very small

FUNDAMENTALS
- Get a mad-on
- The difference between a $100,000 earner and a $25,000 earner is how they feel about what they do
- You win with your heart not your head
- Passion, emotion and excitement are created by:
    - Not liking someone or something. Not liking banks, insurance companies and savings and loans.
    - We hate them all with a passion

CRUSADE
Having a crusade and righting wrongs gives you the extra ounce of courage to do the unthinkable

People don't want to just join a business or a money making operation. They buy into you, your mission, your calling and your mad-on.

AVOID
Avoid the cool, the calm, the deliberate, the sophisticated, the professional, the aloof, the intellectual and the educated. Recruit the wide eyed and enthusiastic

The reason 80% of the people quit is because they think it's just a business.

THE SPIRIT OF ALW
- Form a culture, and an environment that we are a different kind of company for a different kind of person
- You have to talk passionately
- Your crusade has got to cause goose bumps
- Spirit is how you use your body language
- You need to have fire in your eyes and a fire in your belly
- People want to belong to something special

THE PURPOSE OF A PRESENTATION IS TO DISTURB.

WE SELL A POT OF GOLD AT THE END OF A RAINBOW.

A JOB: A NON-OVERRIDE GENERATED INCOME
- Warning, if 100% of your income is from your efforts you will be frustrated
- Unemployed every day
- A limited opportunity to make money

WE SELL
- Unlimited income
- Secure income
- Explosive income

RECRUITING
Is the lifeblood of your business. Without it you die.

RECRUIT OR DIE
You can't turn it on and off. . Everything must be geared to recruiting. Your guidelines, recognition, reports. *It's all you talk about.*

LAW... Recruiting must be the answer to your every problem.

- Slow down in sales comes from a slowdown in recruiting
- You are always one recruit away from an explosion
- Everything you do must lead to a recruit

- Keep them coming and keep them going
- Recruiting is fun, sales is lonely
- You can't just "like" recruiting, you've got to "love it"
- We sell hope, a dream, an opportunity and a chance to Be Somebody
- There's nothing like building a team and seeing a teammate succeed

- Get emotionally involved with your team. Cry, laugh and rejoice with your team.
- To create an explosion you must love it. How do you feel about what you do?

- Nobody will follow a dull, disillusioned, dadgum crybaby
- You've got to hunger to Be Somebody and people will follow you
- This company was built for the studs

RECRUITING IS
- 50% CRUSADE
- 50% Selling THE DREAM

Recruit people who have a hunger for financial freedom and business freedom.

TO BE A GREAT RECRUITER
- You can't be a dud
- People buy you, not the company or the system
- You have to have a big personal dream

RECRUITING
The only way to survive is to recruit. It's the only way to make your business grow.
- Recruiting is a lot of people doing a little bit and a few doing a bunch
- Sell the dream
- Sell the sizzle
- Sell the pot at the end of the rainbow

EVERY PIECE OF FLESH...
Wants financial freedom and business freedom!

Get emotional about what this business has meant to you and your family.

<u>WARNING</u>: KEEP IT SIMPLE. TELL THEM...
- ALW is moving down the track
- We are going to make tons of money
- We don't discriminate
- We will leave you behind.
- This opportunity is for real – We don't sell prestige
- We can change your life

- You can become financially independent here
- We guarantee that you can make it but only if you love it.
- Most people won't make it because they don't love it enough

UNWRITTEN LAW: Life turns out the way you see it turning out

98% of the people do enough to get by. Getting by becomes a way of life. Call me anything but average and ordinary.

ALWAYS BE POSITIVE ESPECIALLY WHEN YOU DON'T FEEL LIKE IT

THE DIFFERENCE BETWEEN WINNING AND LOSING IS THIS MUCH
(Art would separate his thumb and index finger about an inch)

Art Williams: Part 10
WINNING FINANCIALLY BY RECRUITING

9/17/1996

ART WILLIAMS: PART 10
WINNING FINANCIALLY BY RECRUITING

9/17/1996

THIS IS NO GAME WHEN IT COMES TO WINNING
- Either you are or you are not financially independent
- Recruiting: Everything follows recruiting
- Be a recruiting channel
- Recruit from the heart
- Recruit as you go. It becomes a reason to go anywhere.

- The numbers can't beat you and you can't beat the numbers

It's not how you play the game, it's whether you win or lose the game, and RECRUITING IS THE GAME.

When you recruit someone, immediately plug them into something by recruiting under them.

RECRUIT TO YOUR VISION
- People don't recruit because they don't have a vision
- People don't recruit because they don't see a pot at the end of the rainbow
- People don't recruit because they don't want to conquer the world, they are thrilled just to conquer their city
- The goal is not to just be an RVP but to produce RVPs
- Your recruiting mindset never changes when times are good or times are bad. You can never change your basic philosophy on recruiting
- Create a recruiting culture and environment

GENERAL PATTON
Tell people what you want done and they'll figure out a way to get it done

ELITISTS
Elitists believe only the brightest minds deserve all the goodies and a great life.

HARDEST THING IN THE WORLD
- The hardest thing in the world to be is to be positive
- The easiest thing to do in the world is to quit and to give up
- The hardest thing to do is to fight and keep fighting
- It's hard to believe in yourself, to believe that you are special, to believe that you are different and to believe that you're supposed to Be Somebody
- It's hard to fight back
- It's hard to pick yourself up one more time and try one more time
- Whatever you expect, with confidence, happens
- Once you really believe and expect something to happen to you, it will happen

POSITIVE THINKERS WIN, NEGATIVE THINKERS LOSE
- Attitude affects your success in business, your health, your living longer, your family and your stress level
- The single most important thing you can develop in life is a positive winning attitude
- Poor legacy: Bouncing your grandchild on your knee, the child asks you "What did you do? You answer "I just made a living, I just paid my bills on time and I did all right."
- Life beats you down and then you settle for whatever it gives you

WINNERS HAVE ADVERSITY
- Winners have more problems than losers have but the losers think they have more problems than the winners
- All Winners have setbacks to overcome
- Max Cleland a U.S. Senator lost one arm and two legs in the war
- Chuck Colson was in prison and after prison he started prison Fellowship ministries
- Art DeMoss and Stanley Beyer had no college education

BEAT DOWN
- Most men and women have been so abused, so beat down, that they have given up
- Because they're so beat down, they don't work hard
- Because they have been so beat down, their first choice is to always quit

LOSERS LOSE
- Winners win and losers lose
- Give a loser the best support and the best products and they will still lose
- Winners need only a shot at winning and they will win, no matter what the odds

ART'S CRUSADE
- Arrogance of the elite
- The dress for success crowd
- The big time colleges that make you feel stupid if you didn't go there
- The college professors who have never done anything
- 95% of these people look back on their lives and are sad with huge regrets
- They have never accomplished anything important or special

PLAN OF ACTION FOR 30 DAYS
- Take personal responsibility for your life
- Get better or get bitter
- If you have ever been abused, been cheated, or been hurt, forgive and forget
- Stop making excuses
- Stop blaming others and using them as your excuse

Wake up every day and give your wife or husband a kiss and tell them that you love them.

Go wake up your kids, jump in bed with them and tell them they are special and that they are going to do big things with their lives.

Spend one hour in private time every day getting into shape physically, mentally and reading and praying.

HISTORY OF A.L.WILLIAMS

HISTORY OF A.L. WILLIAMS

- Art's father died with a $10,000 whole life policy. Art was 20 years old.

- Art was head football coach at Kendrick High School in Columbus Georgia.

- 1967 - Art's cousin, Ted Harrison, visited with Art at a family reunion and told him about buy term and invest the difference.

- Art went to a PTA meeting and met the father of a football player who worked at ITT Financial Services and sold buy term and invest the difference.

- 1968 - Art worked part-time for two years and earned and saved $40,000 at ITT.

- Lou Miller, his assistant football coach, became Arts first client. Lou became an RVP in AL Williams years later.

- Art hired Bobby Johnson, who hired Tee Faircloth, who hired Bobby Buisson

- They all started part time.

- 1970 - Art moved to Atlanta and went full-time with ITT Financial.

- 1973 - Art moved to Waddell and Reed because there was another level on the computer for his people to start getting overrides.

- 1973 - Art was promoted to RVP in charge of the Southeast region for Waddell and Reed.

- 1976 - Waddle and Reed's parent company, Continental Investment Corporation, filed for Chapter 11 bankruptcy.

- Replacement forms were necessary and took two weeks to get back.

- We had old agent confrontations

- The insurance wars began

- Rusty Crossland was promoted to division manager at Waddell and Reed and Bobby Buisson became the first replacement in the company's history.

- 1977 - February 10, 85 people left Waddell and Reed to start AL Williams.

- The first insurance carrier that worked with us was Financial Assurance from Kansas City, Missouri

- August, 1977 - The president of Financial Assurance said to Art "The deal is off". A.L.WILLIAMS was running them out of money. They couldn't afford all the business that was being written.

- April, 1978 - Bob Turley introduced Art Williams to Boe Adams, who was a wholesaler for National Home Life.

- September, 1979 - The president of National Home Life dies before signing a long term contract with A.L.Williams.

- The board of National Home Life tells Boe Adams to find another company to move our business to.

- February, 1980 - Penn Corp. Financial signs on to be our insurance carrier

- 1986 - Penn Corp. merges with American Can Corporation

- 1988 - American Can changes its name to Primerica Financial Services

- 1989 - Primerica sells to Sandy Weill and Commercial Credit

- 1989 - Art Williams sells A.L.Williams to Commercial Credit which later became Citigroup.

- 4/1/10 - Primerica, Inc goes public on the NYSE

ART'S MEMORABLE QUOTES

ART'S MEMORABLE QUOTES

"Either you are growing or you are dying."

"SIMPLIFY AND MULTIPLY"

"The ones you think will won't and the ones you think won't will."

"Life is just a FLICKER."

"The single most important thing you can develop in life is a positive winning attitude."

"98% of the people do enough to get by. Getting by becomes a way of life for most people."

"Life turns out the way you see it turning out."

"Things are never as good as they seem or as bad as they seem."

"Never get too high or too low."

At every RVP meeting in the early days Art would say "We are probably not going to make it but if we do it will be great."

Someone asked "Art, what if we don't make it, then what?" ART responded, "We will find a hotel room, get a whiteboard, draw a bunch of circles and then find something to put in the circles. We are a distribution company."

"The things that get praised get done."

"I don't promise you it is going to be easy. I just promise you it's going to be worth it."

"Love your people and show it."

"Get a Mad-On"

"I don't know why but my butt is always burning."

"You win with your heart not your head."

"The winners do everything the losers do but they do a little bit more."

"There is no excuse not to be great."

"The WINNERS stay motivated for as long as it takes to get the job done."

"Almost" is a way of life for most people."

"Winners win, losers lose."

"The #1 job of an RVP? To produce growth."

"College professors don't have enough sense to come in out of the rain!"

"People don't care about what you know until they know you really care!"

"There's never been a test that can look inside a man's 'heart'!"

"Dumb! Dumb! Dumb!"

"Winners are MADE, not born!"

"Think BIG!"

"Dream BIG!"

"The MAGIC of 90 days!"

"Successful people do whatever it takes...and a little bit more!"

"Don't let the door hit you in the butt!"

"Don't be phony! People will 'smell' you out."

"Treat people GOOD!"

"We do what's RIGHT!"

"Do it first!"

"Do it, then talk!"

"Body language is the strongest language in the world today. "

"People can spot a phony a mile away."

"Most great people are in a hurry."

"We are probably not going to make it, but if we do we will be big".

Get excited – "No one will follow a dull, disillusioned, dadgum crybaby."

AN ICONS CREED:
"Almost everybody can stay motivated for 2 to 3 months but a winner stays motivated for as long as it takes to get the job done."

"Being a crusader gives you the extra ounce of courage that it takes to win."

"Either you are or you are not financially independent."

"Either you are or you aren't somebody."

"All you can do is all you can do and all you can do is enough."

"Everyone walks around with a neon sign on their chest saying 'Make me feel special."

"I want to Be Somebody so bad it borders on being an obsession."

"One day they will be patting your face with a shovel and on your tombstone will be Dud or Stud…"

"I ain't average."

"Call me anything but average and ordinary"

"The Winners just do it and do it and do it and do it until the job gets done. Then talk about how great it is to Be Somebody that they are proud of and how they are not like everybody else."

"Smart people have a hard time making it in this business."

"This is an endurance contest."

"DADGUMMIT"

"All my life I wanted people to look at me and think I'm special, to say to me "You are a winner."

"No one will deny me my opportunity to win."

"In my darkest hour, I said to myself "you are only one stud away from a surge."

"A person makes a position, a position does not make a person."

"The difference between losing and winning is just a small fraction."

"Making money ELECTRIFIES ME!"

The American people will not follow a pansy, a fence sitter or a mealy-mouth."

"In a hopeless situation, always CHARGE"

"We don't have a job, we have a destiny."

"Go! Go! Go!"

"I don't want to be part of a humdrum existence. I want to make a difference with my life."

"Art, I can't sell my house, what do I do? Just do it."

"There will never be a test that can determine the heart of a man."

"JUST DO IT!"

"You are one RECRUIT away from an explosion and you must believe that RECRUIT is right around the corner."

"Winners stay motivated for as long as it takes to get the job done."

"CRUSADERS die hard"

"You must see yourself involved in something bigger than just your business."

"Have a lot of people doing a little bit and a few people doing a lot."

"I don't promise you it will be easy, I promise you it will be worth it."

"If you keep doing the right things long enough, you will build an empire."

"Being a crusader gives you the extra ounce of courage that it takes to win."

"Two choices to make: Be rich, powerful and meaningful part of this company or be average and ordinary"

"I don't like sales, I like recruiting."

"All my life I wanted to Be Somebody."

"Everything I've done, I'm ashamed of."

"If I could live my life over, I would work harder."

"I was tired of being disappointed in Art Williams."

"I was so sick and tired of second guessing myself, I decided to go for it."

"Selling is not where it's at. I want to be financially independent. I have to build a business to be financially independent."

"For things to get better you get better. For things to change you change. For things to become more positive you become more positive"

Get a "MAD ON"

"I want to Be Somebody so bad, there's nothing I won't do."

"TOTAL COMMITMENT is the first step to greatness."

"We sell a pot of gold at the end of the rainbow."

"The dream: A guy like me, who comes from where I come from, who wants to Be Somebody, is given the chance to go into business for himself, with no education required and where you can build financial independence for your family."

"There has never been a test to measure the heart of a man or a woman."

"There is never a test to see if a person's got the goodies or not."

"This is a company of destiny."

"Push up sales and sales will fall down again. You push up people and sales will stay up forever."

"If we grow to be better people, there's nothing we can't do."

"I want to do something great and record breaking."

"The worst that can happen is that people who produce will make a lot of money."

"I just don't want to be a half-butted, mediocre, average and ordinary organization. I want to do something great. I want this organization to Be Somebody. I want you to Be Somebody."

"The alternative to ALW is just making a living."

"For things to change, you've got to change. For things to get better, you've got to get better."

"Life will give you whatever you are willing to fight for and take."

"You can't just show up to work. You've got to suck it up"

"Make everybody feel special."

"Everyone should be treated as a person you respect and want to be like."

"I want to make a difference in people's lives."

"I wasn't supposed to just exist."

"I wasn't put on this earth to be a half butt."

"I want to be part of something great."

"Some people can stay motivated for 3 to 4 months, good people 6 to 12 months, a stud can remain motivated forever."

"You are one recruit away from an explosion and you must believe that recruit is right around the corner."

ART'S PRESENT DAY FAX MESSAGES

ART'S PRESENT DAY FAX MESSAGES

11/4/16

DO IT ANYWAY

People are unreasonable, illogical and self-centered. Love them anyway

- If you do good, people will accuse you of selfish ulterior motives. Do good anyway
- If you are successful, you will win false friends and true enemies. Succeed anyway
- Honesty and frankness make you vulnerable. Be honest and frank anyway
- The good you do today will be forgotten tomorrow. Do good anyway
- The biggest people with the biggest ideas can be shot down by the smallest people with the smallest pride. Think big anyway
- People favor underdogs but follow only top dogs. Fight for some underdogs anyway
- What you spend years building may be destroyed overnight. Build anyway
- Give the world the best you have and you'll get kicked in the teeth. Give the world the best you've got anyway

READ THE ABOVE EVERYDAY

11/4/16

Napoleon Hill said in his book Think and Grow Rich written in 1937:

"Wishing will not bring the riches, but desiring riches with a state of mind that becomes an obsession, and planning definite ways and means to acquire riches, and backing those plans with persistence which does not recognize failure, will bring riches."

Use these six steps for your financial independence

A COACH

- A coach looks for the good things in all their players
- A coach becomes an expert in praise and recognition

A BOSS
- A boss looks for weakness
- A boss becomes an expert in criticism and intimidation

MONEY

It's not what you earn, but what you keep that counts. – An unwritten law is to always live under your means; save, save, save

11/29/16

Wake up with determination and go to bed with satisfaction

11/30/16

A L Williams was built for people who grew up tough – built for people who were put down and were told they weren't good enough or smart enough by companies, bosses, professors, teachers, and maybe even coaches

ALW WAS BUILT

For the average and ordinary people who wanted to be somebody, that had almost given up, but still had a lot of fight in them and were dreamers.

WE TALKED TOUGH
- This was no game to us
- This was our life
- We all knew coach talk

We ran off:
- The pretty people
- The fancy people
- The three-piece suit people
- CEOs
- Because they all wanted to start at the top and skip steps 1–9

12/3/16

At ALW we knew there was so much more than how much money you can make

- We believed we could change the world
- We believed we could do something important

DOERS

The world needs dreamers and the world needs doers, but above all, the world needs dreamers who do… Are you a doer?

SCREWED

Every player had been screwed, or knew someone who had been screwed by corporate America.

Every player at ALW wanted to hit somebody, pay somebody back or hurt 'em

12/12/16

Took the Dull World of life insurance and made it fun, exciting

A.L.WILLIAMS

Was a team where you:

- Were never alone
- You never go into a strangers home
- You never call strangers or cold prospect
- Never knock on a strangers door

BUILD RELATIONSHIPS

Do your people trust you? – Do your clients trust you

It takes times and most leaders won't spend the time to do it

WE RECRUIT

Coaches

- Teachers

- Doctors
- Lawyers
- Policeman
- Fireman
- Nurses
- The best of the best in your community

12/13/16

HOW TO BUILD A TEAM

Stupid recruiting; to get on the leaders bulletin or to win a contest

DO IT First
- 3 to 4 nights a week across the kitchen table
- When you lose momentum, you go do it, don't tell your team to do it.

To be a great coach you must be passionate – to be passionate you must love it – to keep passion you must never forget the things that blew your butt out of the water.

Make your team better with 4 to 5 pointers ; married, kids, Home, job, 27–55
- Do not recruit professional sales people or insurance agents
- We want crusaders, warriors and fighters

Have a goal of 50% insurance-licensed people – Help your new recruit build a team through field training

Every recruit gets 3 to 4 field training sales/recruits – Never use professional trainers – build field trainers
- Get them securities licensed
- Never bring a prospect to a meeting first
- Always recruit across the kitchen table 1st
- Identify studs
- Build relationships and sell the RVP position.
- Promote someone every month – this keeps the momentum going
- Be a coach not a boss
- Look for the good things in everyone

- Be an expert in praise and recognition
- Draw a map of the USA and Canada then pick the states you want to go to and build.
- Teach everyone the AL Williams way; no cold calling, always work the warm market. You learn best by doing.
- Be tougher than anybody – I can't promise you it's going to be easy, I just promise you it's going to be worth it.
- Compete don't compare
- Always keep expenses low
- Love your people and show it.

12/13/16

- You cannot build a legacy/business without:
- building relationships
- every recruit need someone to care about them
- to tell them how special they are
- to tell them how proud you are of them
- to tell them you love them and you show them you love them
- Mike Tuttle was the best of all the ALW leaders and we had thousands and thousands of great ones.

Art Said:

WISDOM FROM THE COACH

ART SAID: WISDOM FROM THE COACH

Treat everyone as if they have a blinking neon sign on their chest saying "Make me feel special".

I created the ALW Way system because of all my insecurities. I was insecure about:
- A steady paycheck Override system
- I didn't like selling
- I didn't want to be known as a life insurance salesman
- I didn't want to be unemployed everyday and need to make a sale to feed my family
- I didn't want to cold call
- I didn't want to work nights
- I didn't like rejection

My mindset:
- I wanted a business not a job
- I didn't want a limited income
- I needed a secure income
- I needed a crusade
- I needed an enemy

Success is inevitable if you do the right things long enough

Everybody has a flashing sign on their chest that says "make me feel special, make me feel good, say something good to me, I want to Be Somebody."

This is an endurance contest.

Is being respected for what you do important to you?

Coach the person to where you want them to be and not where they are. (You are the best corner back I've ever coached).

Things are never as good as you think they are and are never as bad as you think they are.

We created this business with our hearts.

I don't promise you it will be easy. I promise you it will be worth it. You better be totally committed or you won't survive it.

All the heroes burned all the bridges, rolled the dice, bet everything on their future.

Our Crusade was to correct an injustice.

You are either an RVP or an RVP trainee.

I created the ALW Way system because of all my insecurities about sales, rejection, cold calling, being in the insurance business and recruiting.

90% of winning is being excited.

The ones you think will won't. And the ones you think won't will

Never forget what blew your butt out of the water
- Rule of 72
- Growth through the MULTIPLES
- Making extra money

We sell hope, dreams, and an opportunity.

The Crusade gives you the courage to make a phone call.

Crusaders die hard.

Life is just a flicker.

Build 7-10 Direct RVPs and you will be financially independent.

Building is an all the time thing. It's a mindset .

Attitude is everything.

All I wanted my new recruit to understand is that all they needed to recruit was three, they could get more, but all they needed were three.

You get quality by recruiting quantity.

We created a system whereby recruiting never stops.

We recruit people to go RVP to create a RVP factory.

Life is 10 percent what you make it and 90 percent how you take it.

A team is a group of people working together with one heartbeat!!!!

Rusty Crossland: "Art showed me his weekly override check. It was for $2400! I understood recruiting immediately."

You capture the heart then you capture the man.

You win with your heart not your head.

You show me a husband and wife together in business and I'll show you an Awesome Power!

You are either growing or dying.

There has never been a test nor will they ever be you determine the heart of a man or a woman.

I never told you it would be easy I only told you it would be worth it.

Capture the heart, you've captured the person.

I think it's almost impossible for a smart person to win in business in America today.

Page 202 ALW Way. "A true leader always sets the standard for his people by doing it first. He never asks his people to do anything that he hasn't already done first".

What's the difference between the $50K earner and the $500K earner? ... And a little bit more. It's what I call the winning edge..

Excuses don't count in Life. Excuses don't count in the Big Leagues.

Major league baseball, NFL, NBA isn't the BIG LEAGUES. The BIG LEAGUES IS YOUR LIFE.

You're supposed to Win no matter what happens to you...bad things & good things.

The only thing people remember is what's on the scoreboard.
What's your scoreboard going to read when they click your light out?

You going to BE SOMEBODY, you going to be a WINNER?

Time will tell...

Just do it.

You have a responsibility as a leader in A.L. Williams to make money. You have a responsibility to your people to win…

Just keep calling the plays.

All you can do is all you can do it all you can do is enough.

First step to greatness is total commitment. Are you totally committed?

Building a team is the only way to build wealth that lasts long after you are gone.

Build a company within a company.

To build financial independence, you must recruit 'wide' and 'deep.'

90% of recruiting is being excited.

Our system is to get a lot of people doing a little and a few people doing a lot.

I can't afford to be in sales.

People don't want to sell insurance, they want to override

We are not a sales company, we are a management company. Build teams not salesmen.

I left ITT because Waddell and Reed had another level on the computer, which caused people to recruit and get overrides.

We built this company by creating $3x3x3x3x3x3x3x3x3x10 = 59,000$ RVP'S @ \$10,000 premium per RVP = \$59,000,000 a month in premium. $7x7x7 = \$343,000$ per month in income.

You don't want all your points in the base, you can't multiply there. All your money is made at the 2nd and 3rd generations because of the multiples.

Recruiting is the life blood of your business.

You can solve every problem in your business by recruiting a new person and going 4 deep.

We are not a sales company, we are an override company.

We have no desire to be in the sales business and waking up every day knowing you have to make a sale in order for your family to survive.

The ability to make overrides promotes freedom and overrides come from building a team.

Advantages of our override system are unlimited income/secure income.

When you look in the mirror what do you see?

Your job is to build a company within a company.

It's time to quit running and to quit hiding. It's time to make your stand, to do it or not to do it.

I ain't average.

Life is just a Flicker.

Our company wasn't built for the pretty people.

I want to Be Somebody so bad it borders on being an obsession.

I can never forgive the life insurance industry for what it did to us.

You were put here to make a difference.

The difference between making $100,000 a year and $25,000 a year, is how you feel about what you do.

You've got to get a mad on.

My goal is to create more financially independent people than any company in the world.

If you win in business, if you make a lot of money, and you lose your family you are not a winner.

Art, I can't sell my house. Well, just sell it. But Art, houses aren't selling. Well, sell it anyway. How can you sell your house if houses aren't selling?

I'm an RVP now, can I stop doing it? I'm Financial independent now, can I stop doing it? No! You really have to do it!

The difference between winning and losing is this much. (1 inch).

One day when they will be patting your face with a shovel.

You can't win without a total commitment.

Winners talk about how great it is Be Somebody that they are proud of and how they're not like everybody else.

You can't win the Kentucky Derby with a plow horse.

The NBA, the NFL, major league baseball, they aren't the big leagues. Your life is the big leagues.

No one will follow a dull, dissolutioned, dadgum cry baby.

You need to build 7 to 10; so understand promoting RVPs.

Here's how we built it: 3x3x3x3x

We are an RVP company.

Life won't give you what you want. Life will only give you what you're willing to fight for.

I want to Be Somebody so bad it borders on being in obsession.

On your tombstone will be dud or stud.

I can't stand being average and ordinary. Call me anything but average and ordinary.

I AIN'T AVERAGE!!!

You've got to see yourself involved in something bigger than just your business.

You've got to have a big dream and it's got to be important to you.

My butts always Burning.

Most people can stay motivated for a day, or a week, or a month, but a winner stays motivated for as long as it takes to get the job done. Winners do it and do it and do it.

If you talk recruiting 99% of the time it falls in half. If you talk recruiting 98% of the time it will stop.

You can't wear two hats. We are not a sales company.
The only number I needed to see on a daily basis was how many new recruits came in the day before.

If they shut us down we were just going to go to a hotel meeting room, draw circles and find another product to put in the circle. Because we are a distribution company.

The opportunity lies in the power of building a team.

Larry, you're just not money motivated.

ART'S QUOTES THAT GOT YOU RECRUITING

Company Legends Share Their Favorite
Art Quotes on Recruiting

ART'S QUOTES THAT GOT YOU RECRUITING

LARRY WEIDEL:
"Recruiting is the fastest way from the bottom to the top."

JOHN ROIG:
"ALW was built to give people that look like you and me a chance to become financially independent."
That's the only way to make big money and leave a legacy by building a hierarchy!!!!

JOSH HUFFMAN:
"You are only one recruit away from an EXPLOSION!"
It's like bass fishing, you always think that with the next cast you're going to hook the Big one. It gave me hope, and a sense of anticipation. Our business is a lot like a human lottery, and the more tickets you have, the greater your odds.

FRANK JOYCE:
"And the top 2 percent is a dog fight but most will quit cause they DON'T have the goodies."

JOHN ABER:
"Most won't join but enough will"

BILL WHITTLE:
"You're one recruit away from an explosion!!"
Knowing (or at least believing) that if I kept recruiting, I would, eventually, find that "one" that would start my explosion and the next and the next and the next !!! I also saw it happen in sports!!

MIKE LANDRUM:
"You're one recruit away from an explosion!!!"
Go build new relationships, gives me energy, hope.

WHITNEY COOPER:
Key to winning ...3 words... "Recruit large numbers" ... "Through quantity you find quality."

KIM CARVER:
"I can sum up this business in 3 words: Recruit! Recruit! Recruit!"

CARLOS GONZALEZ:
"You're one recruit away from an explosion."
"The millionaires of tomorrow are barely getting started today."

SAM SHEPHERD:
"...at every level, You are only one or two recruits away from a new surge…"
It gave me Hope that no matter how slow things were going, I was just 1 recruit away from an explosion. Hope is something we all need!!!

COLLIS TEMPLE:
"You've got to keep people coming and going!"
First of all, his level of success and my understanding that his success was directly tied to the company's when he said that; meaning if that's what he was focusing on, it was probably what I needed to be focusing on. Secondly "keep them coming and going" along with "create a system whereby recruiting never stops" led me to believe that I could, once I got big enough and did it the right way for long enough, have a system that continued to grow without my HAVING to be as directly involved!

CHRIS KOOB:
When he talked about walking out of the house and already beating up himself and "then he moved into management". He followed that by talking about recruiting a stud that quit almost immediately, and then another recruit that wouldn't call his warm market ("insurance? Well throw up").
It made me realize that it was just numbers. He had the same obstacles and recruited the same knuckleheads and just kept persevering.

TODD GREER:
"More than 90% of winning is being excited"
"People won't follow a dull, disillusioned, frustrated crybaby"
"I'm not telling you its going to be easy, I am telling you it is going to be worth it"

ART MYERS: (original 85 member)
"All you can do is all you can do and all you an do is enough.

DICK WALKER:
"You're only one recruit away from an explosion in your base shop."

ASAAD FARAJ:
ALL MY LIFE I WANTED TO BE SOMEBODY... WINNERS DO IT AND DO IT AND DO IT TILL THE JOB GETS DONE!
Nobody has or ever will do anything great by themselves.

RANDY GODFREY:
"To have a secure and unlimited income, you must recruit!" and…."ALW is a management company! We build people, not sales."

JON LAVIN:
"You are 1 recruit away from changing your life forever!"
I Understood and accepted the numbers because I knew that if the right person came along that it could start a recruiting explosion! I was 1 person away from a recruiting surge! 1 person from an explosion! It gave me the courage to talk to everyone! He said that everybody had a flashing sign on their chest that said " make me feel special!"

FRANCES AVRETT:
"You are one recruit away from an explosion!"
I wanted to build 7 to10 key leaders (Giants) to become stone wealthy! That is the formula Art gave us. So I kept recruiting to find my 7 to 10.

ANDY YOUNG:
"You're either growing or you're dying!"
Many people feel that growing/dying is ominous or threatening in some way. A key to LIFE and LIVING is living or moving water vs. still/stagnant. The sooner we submit to growing by recruiting, and that we MUST feed the Beast, put fuel in the car in order to live and grow, the sooner we continue to live and grow. It is a total positive!

DAVID FARMER:
"You are one recruit away from Explosion".
It always kept me believing that every day was a new day and I was always afraid someone else would find them before I did.

MARY RANDALL WALKER:
"All you have to do is build 7-10 first generation RVPS & teach them to do that...& you'll become financially independent!"
We wanted those 7-10 as soon as possible...so we SOLD THE HECK out of that promise of getting 7-10 to every single recruit...that THEY could be an RVP, too!! AND IT WORKED!!
We didn't RECRUIT TO RECRUIT, we RECRUITED to get RVPS!!

BOB SAFFORD:
"Create a system whereby recruiting never stops."

TONIA POE:
"You are one recruit away from an explosion."
My up-line Neal didn't know a $500,000 earner like me was coming, but he BELIEVED I was.

NICK ALISE:
"You are 1 recruit away from an explosion" and "You are growing or you are dying!"
 It's the only way to build 7-10 real 1st generation RVPs!

MARIO ARIZON:
"Don't let the whiners and the complainers change you make you sour make you quit. You are a winner. You're a leader, you are a coach, you're a motivator. Let me tell you what you're not. You ain't no banker you ain't no psychiatrist"

MIKE TUTTLE:
Art said that we were building a management company that would provide me with unlimited security and unlimited income. Well the income did not hit me nearly as hard as the word SECURITY. I wanted security for my family. I wanted protection for them in case I got sick, injured, died. And obviously to build a management company that would provide my family security I had to recruit a lot of people. So I did. I can still so clearly remember when I had my stroke. Until they could run all kind of tests, I did not know what my working future looked like. But I remember very clearly how thankful I was that I had already built a giant team that would provide security for my family even if I could never work again.

MARK MARCHESANI:
"Some people can stay motivated for 2 or 3 months, some for 2 or 3 years, but a winner stays motivated for 20 or 30 years or for however long it takes to win!"
It kept me recruiting when people quit and kept me in the hunt recruiting when I felt like quitting.

JOE TANSEY:
"You're one recruit away from an explosion!"
That next recruit can take you 3 months 3 years or get you total financially independent ......That's what keeps me having a recruiting mindset vs. looking for sales !!
Also: "Leaders who build a big base shop and keep producing first generation RVPs.....then those leaders get the greatest honors and greatest rewards."

JIM PENN:
"In fact, we have built our company in such a manner so that the ONLY way you can succeed is by Pushing Up People "
This spurred me on because we wanted to build a great business and to become financially independent. I looked at Art as the master builder and

believed if we focused on what he said, recruiting & pushing up people, we'd achieve our goals!

BOBBY GOCOOL:
"You are always one recruit away from an explosion!"

BOBBY BUISSON:
"You're only ONE RECRUIT from an explosion!"
It's my favorite because it worked for me. After recruiting Ron Wright then Al Paracci our biz took off. I became #1 District and recruiter in the company.

ART'S WAY : THE A.L.W. SYSTEM
The Definitive and Timeless Way to Build Your Business

THE ALW SYSTEM
The Definitive and Timeless Way to Build Your Business

There's no better measurement tool than the bottom line. Think of the bottom line as the end, the take away, the desired result.

Create a better life: For millions of orphans, widows, retirees and a 1% from 100s income life (overrides)

A.L.WILLIAMS - A WARM MARKET COMPANY
#1 - Recruit a part-timer with a warm market
#2 - The recruit's job is to set up the appointment
#3 - The recruit drives you so you don't get lost
#4 - You go in the back door of their best friends house
#5 - The recruit cheerleads the system
#6 - The sale can NEVER be just one appointment
#7 - You recruit the best friend and their best friends
#8 - The best friend sets up an appointment
#9 - You do this over and over again

We don't believe in cold calling, talking to strangers, going to a stranger's home

A.L.WILLIAMS WAS BUILT BY BEST FRIENDS
Always…talking to friends
Always…having a friends "best friend" go with you to the friends house
Always…having the friend set-up the appointment

FOUR PRIORITIES
1. Always make money
2. Develop 7–10 key people
3. Work the law of large numbers in the shortest period of time
4. Develop a system whereby recruiting never stops

CURRENT WAY vs. ALW WAY: The difficulty lies not so much in developing new ideas as in escaping from the old ones. The greatest enemy to tomorrow's success is sometimes today's success. Don't get satisfied. Get creative an build.

WHAT'S YOUR DREAM
- Does it include others?
- How many? Just a few or thousands?

THE POWER OF FOCUS
- No one succeeds by being a generalist
- Have focused, laser thinking
- One mind. Not scattered.
- Make a conscious choice to neglect unimportant things and to focus attention on your profession
- Be SELECTIVE
- Identify your priorities
- "You will become as small as your controlling desire, as great as your dominant aspiration."
- Think on only ONE THING
- Remove Distractions
- W. Clement Stone: "Keep your mind off the things you don't want by keeping it on the things you do want."
- Insulate yourself from distraction
- Multitasking: Are you focused on selling products or recruiting/building RVPs?
- Jack of all trades or Master of none?
- Ralph Waldo Emerson: "Concentration is the secret of strength in politics, in war, in trade, in short in all management of human affairs."
- You cannot be all things to all people
- "Do well at a few things, give up many things."
- You can't know everything and win
- Wandering generalities or steely-eyed specific goals?
- To keep focused: Identify a final destination; an objective
- Maintain your priorities
- Eat, sleep, drink recruiting and RVP promotions
- Strive for Excellence in one thing - Winning
- I have wholesalers to close sales for me. Why do I need to know what they know?
- What area has the greatest impact on my future? On the future of others? Recruiting and building have the greatest impact.
- "Am I dedicated to removing distractions and mental clutter so that I can concentrate with clarity on the real issue?"
- Big Goals: Number of 1st, 2nd, 3rd etc RVPs
- "You don't have goals—or your goals don't align with your dreams—then your focus will get off track."
- Recognize people. Make them feel special. Believe in your people.

ART AT THE 2013 CONVENTION
- We Found a BETTER WAY to build a company. Sales come from recruiting.
- We were Big Dreamers and Big Doers
- How do you expand from 85 to 250,000? The ALW plan was to grow by MULTIPLICATION.

- All you need to know is 3. Recruit 3 @ 10x is 30 people. Recruit 3 who recruit 3 x 10 is 59,000 people.
- At the top of a warm market list are best friends...the bottom is just casual acquaintances
- I recruited Bobby Johnson, who recruited Tee Faircloth, who recruited Bobby Buisson, who recruited Randall Walker. Bobby recruited Bob Miller....all of them brought me 4,000 RVPs, 250,000 licensed people, in all states
- RVP? Many just build a Base Shop to a make living but income stops when you die.
- Be an RVP factory and you build great wealth
- THE DREAM? I wanted to:
    - Be my own BOSS....
    - Be totally financial independent
    - Do something I was passionate about.... I loved it.
    - I wanted a great quality of life. I wanted to have it all.
    - Not having to run a base shop forever or having to recruit greenies.

PHASES OF SUCCESS
- Phase 1 Bust your butt
- Phase 2 Promote RVPs
- Phase 3 They promote RVPs
- Phase 4 Begin to travel and have a great life....

RECRUIT DEEP AND RECRUIT WITH SIMPLICITY
- Only way to find quality is finding quantity
- We have asystem where recruiting never stops. Best friends recruiting best friends and creating 3x3x3x3. It is the only way.
- Have a simple and transferable system
- "Precision is the enemy of simplicity."
- Train on sales or train on how to build a business with 3x3

WE ARE AN RVP COMPANY
- The starting line is RVP by getting a team of 5 direct teams doing 5 sales each
- I'm becoming a "Regional Vice President," not just a "City" Vice President. We have to think bigger. Stay away from "average" thinking.
- Get 7-10 direct RVPs. Help your RVPs get 7-10 RVPs. Those RVPs get 7-10 RVPs.
- Have a minimum of 5 direct-teams to you at ALL TIMES
- Recruit large numbers of 4-5 pointers to accomplish this
- Get 50% licensed

BUILD WITH THE RIGHT PEOPLE
- We build with quality; 4-5 pointers; 90% right market.
- ALW is a warm market company
- Part time concept to start. This allows you to recruit THE CREAM OF THE CROP.

3 STEPS
1. You recruit a best friend
2. Part-timer calls best friend and books appointment. Get part-timer in the field
3. Never sell on first interview because it is stupid

- ALW was built with husband and wife teams. All great teams are husbands and wives building it together.
- Our goals were impossible. Attack the largest industry.
- In 1977, 90% all insurance sold was whole life
- 12 years later we went from 85 people to 250,000 people
- The top 100 insurance companies vs. ALW - We only had 85 people. They had 450,000. We recruited. They didn't.

THE SECRET
- Corporate America believed only special people, degreed people and only pretty people can make it
- In ALW, our people had the heart to win and the desire to Be Somebody
- People were the key to our success
- Teach your new recruit how to build a team
- The GOLD MINE is OVERRIDES: Everybody wants to override.
- What I wanted a new recruit to know is "All you need to recruit is 3!!!"
- Most everybody can think of 3 people
- 3-9-27-81 to 59,000 (compounding people)
- Recruiting surge leads to licensing surge
- A real recruit leads to licensing
- Recruit somebody to get them licensed
- I don't promise you it will be easy. I promise it will be worth it
- Almost is a way of life for most people
- Winners do it and do it and do it
- They do it to be financially independent, to Be Somebody, to be wealthy

The primary difference between winners and losers? Winners do it until the job gets done.

Don't expect to be making big MONEY if you are not willing to recruit BiG.

Jimmy Meyers BROUGHT 3 PEOPLE to a MEETING because he was TOLD to in the OPPORTUNITY MEETING.

THE BIG VISION WE BELIEVED IN
- We were born to change an industry; Born to beat Prudential
- David vs Goliath
- Born to destroy whole life insurance
- ALW was born for people to build their own company within a company
- Built for people that look like me
- To build total financial independence
- Be in a position where nobody can put their thumb on you, where nobody can squeeze you
- Where you are your own boss
- To build real security for your family

EVERYONE WAS BORN TO BE SOMEBODY.
EVERYONE WANTS TO BE SOMEBODY!
- What kind of people were the original people? 3 Things the original ALW people wanted:
    1. Be their own boss
    2. Control their own destiny, where no one can put their thumb on you and squeeze you and control you
    3. And to believe passionately in what they do

You must believe you were born for this.

Motto of ALW: "Everybody wants to Be Somebody."

The Wright Brothers knew of the ENGINE and knew of the GLIDER. They WANTED TO FLY. Their genius was that they were industrious to PUT THE TWO TOGETHER TO FLY and changed the world for BILLIONS of people.

Art Williams knew of BUY TERM AND INVEST DIFFERENCE. He also knew of 3x3x3(1%-100). He wanted to MASS MARKET "buy term and invest the difference" and CREATE FINANCIAL INDEPENDENCE THRU OVERRIDING. He put the two together and brought both to the world.

I run an RVP factory? Do you?

People don't think they know enough people. The Rule of 3 answers that! (3x3x3 etc.)

BUILDING A TEAM
- This is your moment. This is your chance. This is why you were born.
- Multiplication occurs when everyone buys into the system.
- Getting RVPs who go and get RVPs was our CULTURE.
- One heartbeat.
- Only the ALW WAY.
- Can't be looking for a quicker, better way. The system works.
- We were not a sales company where you are unemployed everyday
- If I had a chance to build a business I wanted a BIG INCOME
- The Power of building a Team? Override hundreds and thousands of people.
- Every waking moment all I thought about was building a team.
- Show recruits how to build a team. Start with 3 and drive 4 deep.
- The gold mine is overrides and growing with multiplication not addition.

Overrides are the lure to catch the BIG FISH.

- People want a goldmine that is overriding people
- 3-9-27-81-243-729 = 59,000 people
- Most people recruit then run back to sales
- You must make a total commitment to recruit to get the multiples

WHY BUILD A TEAM
- Unlimited Income
- Secure Income
- Get the recruiting language down
- It is an RVP Factory that creates endless RVPs
- Personal attitude plus effort equals SUCCESS

- Understand the truth that everybody wants to make money off of other people

RVP IS THE STARTING LINE
- At RVP is when you get chance to build your own company
- You are your own boss
- You were put on this earth to build RVPs.

3 FOCUSED GOALS
- Be an RVP
- Build 7-10 RVPs
- Help your RVPs build 7-10 RVPs

New recruits want to know "Where do you see me in 3 years?"

WHERE TO FIND 7-10 RVPS?
The only way is recruiting large numbers. You get quality by hiring quantity.

GIVE EVERY PERSON A CHANCE TO MAKE IT
- How? Multiplication.
- Funnel large number of people thru it. BIG NET to get 3x3.
- The ONLY thing Art thought about was building a TEAM

How did Art get people to leave big money jobs and follow him? His BIG VISION FOR THEM.

Are you a contract RVP or are you PRODUCING RVPS? An RVP contract without a team steals the dream.

People WON'T STICK without a team to override.

Bob Miller:

CHARACTERISTICS OF ART'S MANAGEMENT TECHNIQUES

BOB MILLER ON ART WILLIAMS:
CHARACTERISTICS OF ART'S MANAGEMENT TECHNIQUES

- Never criticize others
- Of all the prisoners on death row, not one of them thought they were wrong. They blame the environment, etc.
- There is no such thing as constructive criticism

Keep selling the dream. You can praise them 1 million times and criticize them just once and they'll remember that forever. Just don't do it. It kills people.

- Praise, praise, praise
- Make them feel good all the time
- Art never gives constructive criticism
- Work with people in a positive way
- Make other people feel important, special, appreciated
- Your people need to see you're looking out for them first
- Care about your people

- Be able to arouse enthusiasm in others
- Have a sincere appreciation and encouragement of your people
- Don't be a phony
- You must make it a way of life

- Be genuinely interested in other people, by being a good listener. Art is a fabulous listener.
- Remember people's names. Art is a fabulous people person. He works hard at it.
- Avoid arguments: you can never win an argument
- Never argue
- Show respect for the other man's opinion

- You can't crush people
- If you are wrong, admit it quickly
- Just get the job done, great signs of leadership is to admit it
- Begin in a friendly way. Art is always positive on the phone.
- Let the other person feel the idea is theirs.

- Give people the freedom to perform. RVPs are building their own business.
- Try to see things from the other persons point of view
- Try to put yourself in other people shoes. What if you had done that to me?

Dramatize your ideas. Make things come alive. Throw down a challenge. Make a competition out of it.

- If you must find fault, begin with honest appreciation
- Give personal examples of your shortcomings first. "You can't make any more mistakes than I have made." Look for the good in people.

Look at your people as winners and champions.

- Be honest and have some integrity, don't be selfish
- I can't be an Art Williams, I can only be me. That is your greatest asset.
- Build your strengths, bury your weaknesses

If you try to be anyone else you'll fail. You can't be someone else. But most of us are afraid to be ourselves.

- Give the credit for success to others. You'll get the ultimate success when you pass around the accolades. Praise the slightest and every improvement.

Give people a fine reputation to live up to. "I knew you would perform". "I knew you would be excellent". "I know you'll be number one and win".

- Art had a sense of urgency to take action
- Have emergency meetings
- Share the latest ideas of this great corporation
- Lead by example. The greatest single thing you can do is lead by example. You do it first.

- Be more positive than anyone else you know
- Plan not to fail
- Think through all the little things
- I think BIG

Don't major in minor things.

- Believe you were meant to be and destined to be a winner

Master the art of recognition. You can never do it too much.

The primary responsibility you have is to make people feel good.

- Don't try to impress others. Let others impress you.
- Art always made me feel special
- Be enthusiastic. Have sincere enthusiasm.

- Be a sincere crusader. Build on people's strengths and uniqueness.
- Don't try to change people
- Make them feel good about themselves

- Always be positive. Always be positive.
- Make people feel better about themselves
- We can elevate peoples self-concept. We mold their self-worth.

Be able to tolerate the imperfections of others. We all think we are the center of the universe.

- Be a master communicator
- Build personal relationships. The best way is to have sincere recognition.
- Look at our business as a miniature A.L.Williams company. The only difference is time.
- When you hear something good about someone, pass it on.
- We are on a pedestal in our peoples eyes
- Have patience. Give your efforts time to compound

Art Williams:

HAVING A GREAT PARTNERSHIP IN MARRIAGE

ART WILLIAMS:
Having a Great Partnership in Marriage

BE THE PERFECT PARTNER
- Can't ever look at your partner as a dud, a loser, or even show doubt
- Work hard for their support
- Be totally committed to them
- Divorce is no option
- This is my business for life. In all areas,. All facets, and all defeats become minimized because of that decision.
- Show it, be happy, show the world you are happy and you love life
- Be a motivator to your spouse by making money and selling them the Dream
- The best way is to praise them, praise them, praise, praise
- Love them:
    - Overflow with love
    - Be affectionate
    - Be loving
    - Be a touching person
- Say I love you often
- There are 1 million different ways to sincerely show it
- Have a honeymoon every 4–6 weeks
- Never criticize them and avoid arguments
- Share a big dream together because it gives you energy
- Have a vision that causes you to fight the fight for them
- Do things together
- Be a great father and mother; love your children
- Be the first to say I'm sorry
- Be a great lover
- Pray a prayer before every meal
- Pray together for your people by name and pray for your business success
- Compliment your partner to change them and not criticize them to change them
- Be excited about seeing each other and show it
- Share financial goals
- Understand that sometimes a good crisis pulls you together.
- Your spouse is the most important person in your hierarchy. Tell her this every day.

LOCKER ROOM NOTES WORD STATISTICS

How many times a certain key word is mentioned in this book can provide you with insight and focus. The Top 5 are in bold lettering.

"Recruit" or "Recruiting" - 382 times

"Dream" - 179 times

"Goal" - 97 times

"Sales" - 116 times

"Insurance" - 51 times

"Build" - 278

"Win" or "Won" - 635 times

"Lead" - 229 times

"Attitude" - 122 times

"RVP" - 168 times

"Love" - 114 times

"Team" - 123 times

"Special" - 95 times

"Lose" or "Loser" - 84 times

"Money" or "Income" - 220 times

"Be Somebody" - 126 times

"Tough" or "Toughness" - 109 times

"Do It" - 151 times

"Desire" - 56 times

"Heart" - 64 times

"Smart" or "Talent" - 28 times

"Commit" or "Commitment" - 102 times

"Family" - 84 times

"Proud" or "Pride" - 86 times

"Dumb Asses" - 2 times

"Convince" - 0 times

Art & Angela Williams

Art and Angela are one of the most fun, dynamic and loving couples I have ever known.
Art said from the beginning "If you win in business, but lose your family, you ultimately will lose."
In a corporate world where family wasn't important, the partnership of spouses in ALW was an important focus and encouraged. They built a company for people to have a family business that would bring financial independence for generations. Art and Angela championed an environment of togetherness, a oneness where each spouse had a valuable part in building a common dream. They modeled an amazing partnership that impacted thousands of marriages and businesses in ALW.
Their philosophy was that two ordinary people, who love each other and have a common goal, can accomplish great and lasting things.

Boe & Mirna Adams

Boe always said "It doesn't cost anything to think big, but it costs everything to think small." He taught us all to think big and had zero tolerance for thinking small. Boe was definitely the smartest man in the room when it came to negotiating with insurance carriers. Our company was limited only by the funding it took to pay the field and Boe never let us down.
Boe knew his numbers. He was a math genius that was ahead of the curve. He knew what the field needed to grow exponentially.

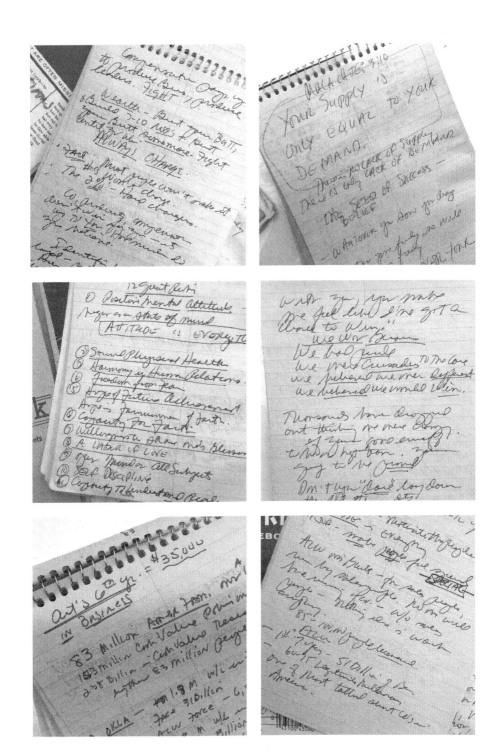

Let us not become weary in doing good, for at the proper time we will reap a harvest if we do not give up.
                                     Galatians 6:9

Ordering information for special discounts or bulk purchases, please contact:

teamorender@me.com

Made in the USA
Middletown, DE
01 June 2017